Modern Japan Through
Its Weddings

Modern Japan Through Its Weddings

Gender, Person, and Society in Ritual Portrayal

WALTER EDWARDS

STANFORD UNIVERSITY PRESS

STANFORD, CALIFORNIA

Stanford University Press
Stanford, California
© 1989 by the Board of Trustees of the
Leland Stanford Junior University

Printed in the United States of America

Original printing 1989

Last figure below indicates year of this printing:

99   98   97   96   95   94   93   92   91   90

CIP data appear at the end of the book

To my parents

Acknowledgments

To the many people and institutions who aided my efforts in producing this work, I offer these expressions of gratitude in partial repayment for the boundless debt I have incurred.

Financial support for the initial field study was provided in 1982–83 by the Japan Foundation and the Social Science Research Council, in the form of a Doctoral Dissertation Fellowship. Robert J. Smith, James A. Boon, and Kathryn March were all instrumental in shaping the Ph.D. dissertation that resulted in 1984. Subsequent advice on the dissertation and its several revisions was kindly offered by Melinda Babcock, Jody Chafee, Paul Dresch, and William Kelly. I am also indebted to an anonymous reader for insights into the nature of Shinto ceremony.

The task of reshaping the manuscript into its present form was aided by a grant from the Center for Japanese Studies of the University of Michigan. I also did some of the rewriting while I was a Visiting Assistant Professor at the Japan Studies Program of the University of Washington. Portions of the book previously appeared in an essay, "The Commercialized Wedding as Ritual: A Window on Social Values," in the *Journal of Japanese Studies*, 13(1) (1987): 51–78.

Like every ethnographer, I am most indebted to my informants, who wittingly or not provided me time and again with bits and pieces of experience lived and remembered—the very materials that make anthropological study possible. In particular, I wish to thank the personnel of White Crane Palace, the wedding hall where I gathered much of the information for this study, for their willingness to serve as my teachers, co-workers, informants, and friends during the time I spent there. I am especially grateful to the managing director (*shihainin*) and to the head of the weddings department (*kankonka*) for opening doors for me that, but for their sympathetic support, would have surely remained shut.

W.E.

Contents

Modern Japan Through Its Weddings

Introduction

"Americans are selfish"—the words irritated me every time Tomiko used them. But during my first few years in Japan she used them often.

I had come to Japan in the early 1970s, shortly out of college. For the next six and a half years I lived in a city I shall call Hirayama, a provincial center of several hundred thousand inhabitants. Most of its populace is densely packed into a flat nucleus barely ten kilometers across; the rest occupies upland valleys stretching far into the nearby mountains, areas that have only come under Hirayama's administration since the war. The local economy, traditionally focused on agricultural produce, now features a number of light industries as well.

The city's prominence in the region dates from a powerful sixteenth-century warlord's decision to locate his castle there, prompting a spurt of urban growth whose impact remains visible in the city's older neighborhoods. Entire districts, built to house the warlord's vassals and their families near the castle walls, still bear names like Castle South and Castle East, or the Inner Castle area nestled between the two moats. To the west one also finds streets such as Carpenter, Sawyer, Dyer, and Draper, named after the artisans and merchants once gathered there to supply their samurai rulers with the necessities of everyday life. Other streets, like Wainwright and Falconer, tell of needs deriving from the samurai's military status. Among the townsmen who provided these services were my maternal ancestors. Knowledge of their origin is now lost, but their direct descendants—the Shimazakis—still live on Swordsmith Street and claim the family had indeed once specialized in the manufacture of scabbards. They also remember the many fine examples of the sword-making craft the house used to possess, before its destruction in the wartime bombings. Of course by then the family had long abandoned that trade for their present one of selling *butsudan,* the Buddhist altars used for ancestral rites in the home.

It was the knowledge of our common ancestry that had brought me to Hirayama. Like many of my generation, I was looking for my roots, seeking to recover some of the heritage my immigrant grandparents had left behind in their desire to assimilate. Yet surely I must have presented an alien figure to the Shimazakis when they met me at Hirayama station: a blue jean–clad American youth, toting a guitar and a backpack, barely able to ask directions after one summer's study of the language. I was nevertheless greeted warmly by Ken'ichi and Tomiko, who loaded me into their car for the short drive home.

Shimazaki Saki, my maternal grandmother, had left Hirayama sixty years earlier to attend college in San Francisco. There she met and married a fellow countryman who had no intention of returning to Japan. Determined even to avoid living among Japanese in his adopted homeland, he and Saki moved from the West Coast and eventually settled in a small southern town, where my mother and her siblings grew up learning nothing of their parents' native language. All contact with our Japanese relatives thus ended with my grandmother's death in the late 1960s, some twenty-five years after her husband's. "When the letters stopped coming, we assumed she had died," Saki's younger brother Keisuke told me. He had taken over the family business soon after his sister's departure, seeing it through a period of crisis in the 1920s and later rebuilding it from scratch after the war. Only once, in 1959, did Saki return for a visit, her pace already hampered by failing health. The Shimazakis were thus prepared for the silence that fell less than a decade later.

I was not the first to break that silence. Two years earlier my sister had come to Japan, carrying a letter we had found among Saki's belongings. From the return address she managed to contact the Shimazaki household in Hirayama and paid a visit before going back to America. This made my own journey considerably easier. I knew not only where I was going, but who I would meet: Keisuke, retired from active life but still commanding deference as the nominal household head; Fumie, his wife of fifty years; their son Ken'ichi, now in charge of the business; Tomiko, the daughter-in-law, who actually saw to much of the store's day-to-day management; and the two teen-aged grandchildren.

My arrival occasioned an extended celebration, a round of feasts with the Shimazakis and more distant relations. As at all family gatherings, photographs bridged the gulfs of time and distance. There was my grandmother as I had never known her, the portrait dating from her final year in school—back then only seniors were allowed to tie up their hair like that, I was told. Saki and two classmates sported the same billowing hairstyle: had the schoolgirl friends posed on learning of her departure, knowing they might never meet again? Other pictures had been sent back from America: a sepia-toned portrait of Saki as a fashionable young woman, moonlike face peering from under the wide brim of a feathered hat; a snapshot of Saki beside the family car after a rare snowstorm hit their southern home; another of her matronly form dressing a Thanksgiving turkey ("look at how *big* it is!"). More pictures from the Shimazakis' album told of her Hirayama visit. "There we are in the temple garden together," said Tomiko, pointing to an image of herself with an infant strapped to her back. "Gee, had I already gained so much weight by then?" In another picture I recognized a coat I had worn as a child. "Saki sent over so many things during those years after the war," recalled Keisuke, "food, clothes, money . . . We had so little, only 200 yen at war's end, the house and store in ashes." Neither he nor Fumie could talk of those times without coming to tears. Clearly they felt an *on*, an unrepayable debt of gratitude, to Saki for the help she had given. And just as clearly that feeling warmed the welcome I received. It all made discovering my roots an unexpectedly easy and pleasant experience.

But I had also come to stay, and to my relatives that was a different matter. What would I do? Where would I live? When did I plan to go back?

"Uorutā"—I had not been given a name easily rendered in the Japanese tongue—"you can't stay in Japan too long, you know."

"Why not?"

"You should be home. You're the eldest son. Who's going to look after your parents?"

"They can look after themselves. Besides, 'eldest son' doesn't mean the same thing in English." Indeed, I had never thought of myself as an "eldest son" precisely because our term lacks the notions of special rights and duties that mark its Japanese equivalent.

"So what happens to your parents when they get too old to care for themselves?"

This being a question Americans prefer to avoid, I change the subject. "But how else can I learn about Japan?"

"What will you do—learn Japanese and then go home and teach it?"

"No, I just want to stay here for a while. I don't know what I'll do when I go back, if I go back. I'm not worrying about it yet."

"You see, Americans are selfish! Always thinking of themselves!"

Selfish or not, my intentions were taken more seriously by the Shimazakis once I found work, rented an apartment, and settled into the daily routine that I maintained for the next several years. My job of teaching English at a private language school involved only my evenings, so in the morning I sat home studying Japanese. By midday, hungry for both food and human contact, I headed for the Shimazakis'. There I would usually find some task to perform for the store that afternoon—most often helping with the delivery of a butsudan to a customer's home.

What a marvelous excuse to peek into the households in and around Hirayama! There were tiny three-room apartments of urban *danchi* dwellers. There were homes of shopkeepers like the Shimazakis themselves, with cramped living quarters built over a ground-level store—no choice here but to bring the butsudan in through the store entrance and up narrow stairs often cluttered with merchandise. There were other urban structures used strictly for residence, although most still required two stories to make best use of lots so tiny that one-fortieth of an acre was considered reasonable. And then there were the homes of farmers in the outlying districts, who seemed the only ones blessed with all the room they wanted. Although the old-style farmhouses are quite small—four adjoining rooms plus a large entry and kitchen—they are linked to several outbuildings by a zone that doubles as work area and garden. Newer houses are both larger and of more modern design. But they retain features that still distinguish them from most city homes, like a hallway along the south side that opens verandalike onto the garden.

They are also more likely to have a separate alcove provided for the butsudan.

"Farmers have lots of money for such things nowadays, with land prices as high as they are," Ken'ichi once remarked. "They also care about their ancestors, so when they build a new house they often buy a new *butsudan* too. That's where our best sales come from." But sometimes the delivery was to an older farmhouse, where placing the butsudan directly on the tatami mats caused it to lean forward, its cabinet doors swinging open from their own weight. "The tatami gets worn down toward the center, so you have to wedge something under the front of the *butsudan* to keep it level. Ask them for a piece of wood. The wife may have some *kamaboko* [a fish pâté molded on top of a thin block of wood] in the kitchen; the board is usually just the right thickness. And the husband always stashes odd scraps of wood under the floor to the left of the entry."

If getting involved in the Shimazakis' work meant learning about their customers' living habits in detail, it provided opportunities for learning other things as well.

"Now, the Japanese language is interesting, isn't it?" Tomiko commented one day en route to a customer's house. "Take counting words, for instance. There are so many that young people don't bother to learn them these days. Do you know the proper way to count chests of drawers?"

In a manner vaguely resembling our use of "gaggles" for geese and "schools" for fish, the Japanese count virtually everything with nominals that classify the object in question. I had learned, for example, that butsudan are counted as *hon*—the same counter used for pencils or other items longer in one dimension than in others. Five butsudan are thus *butsudan go hon*.

I guess by analogy. "Is it *hon*?"

"Wrong! It's *sao*. What about dressers? They're *men*—it's the mirror that's really being counted, and they're treated as surfaces [*men*]. Young people would just count mirrors as *mai*, but they're really *men*." Mai is a general counter for flat objects, like paper, boards, or plates. I conclude that much of the complexity of the language exists so that adult speakers can show their erudition to socially deficient people like foreigners and children.

But the hardest lesson of all was seeing how, in the Shimazakis' eyes, I *was* a child.

"Uorutā, you should be thinking about buying a house, you know."

The Shimazakis had accepted that I would stay in Japan, perhaps forever. That did not lessen their concern about my behavior, as Tomiko's remarks showed.

"Why? I'm too young to worry about such things now."

"But that's just the problem. In Japan you'll never really be seen as an adult until you're married and buy a house. No one will trust you unless you do. At the very least you've got to marry. But having a house makes a real difference. People won't suspect you of doing something bad—you can't run away and hide if you've got a house to dispose of. And buying the house first would make it really easy to get a bride. Lots of girls would marry you in a flash if you had a house."

I protested vigorously. I had no desire to marry someone only interested in a house; Tomiko's comments hardly agreed with my view of marriage as an emotional bond between two people. But if it was a long time before I could listen to such advice with equanimity, my difficulty is understandable, given the magnitude of cultural difference such statements entailed. Of the wide spectrum of things alien to the Western experience in Japanese society, some are far easier to accept than others: we look favorably on the practice of taking off our shoes in the home, for instance, and take pleasure in the challenge of eating exotic foods with chopsticks. But confronting values that challenge our most deeply cherished notions of what it is to be a person is an entirely different matter. I had come to Japan at the age of twenty-three and considered myself an adult. To me, moreover, this meant nothing less than having autonomy as an individual, a condition I regarded as morally proper for an adult in any society.

But my life in Japan brought challenge to those convictions from every quarter. One day as I walked along Exchange Street, where merchant brokers had once conducted financial services approximating those of modern-day banks, I was greeted by a vaguely familiar face.

"Ah! Shimazaki-san, good morning!"

My smile and return salutation, accompanied by the requisite bow, now came automatically. Having completed my part in this routine social skit, I was left free to wonder, as I walked on, precisely who the woman was. Less than a block later I recalled a nearby house where I had helped Ken'ichi with a recent delivery. The person I greeted just now was the same middle-aged housewife who had remarked how unusual it was for a foreigner to be bringing their butsudan. Not only was I unusual, and thus more easily remembered, but I was remembered as a Shimazaki! Of course it is common enough for Japanese workers to be called by their employer's or company's name, and my having been introduced as a relative made such identification all the more plausible. But that hardly lessened the implications of being called Shimazaki-san.

By now those implications needed little explanation.

"Look at what it says here," Ken'ichi had once declared, peering at the newspaper spread before him on the tatami mats of the Shimazakis' home. "This happens almost every year. Some school's withdrawing from the baseball tournament because one of its students was caught shoplifting." Held twice yearly on a national scale, the high school baseball tournament is both athletic competition and highly ritualized drama. With each game, one region's team advances to the next round while another is eliminated. At game's end both victors and vanquished, followed closely by television cameras, play out opposite roles of a standard script: the winners line up at home plate to sing their alma mater, then rush to greet their cheering fans; the losers squat in front of their dugout, tearfully gathering bags of the stadium's dirt to take home as souvenirs. Occasionally, a school principal or coach will decide that a recent scandal precludes his team from participating honorably. Its members then make a symbolic appearance at the tournament's outset before leaving, their tears as they collect their souvenir dirt no less genuine for having lost their chance to play.

"She won't be able to show her face in town anymore," continued Ken'ichi, referring to the shoplifter. To an American the offenses typically involved seem minor; two similar occasions were prompted by students smoking cigarettes and drinking beer. It is all the more remarkable that such incidents are so rare, testimony to how effectively the notion of collective responsibility constrains conduct. To have an identity as a Japanese, then— whether as a student or a member of a family or a firm—means one's actions are no longer fully one's own.

It may be objected that the same notions operate in our society as well. Often enough a worker's individuality is submerged beneath the corporate identity; children are frequently admonished that their actions reflect on their parents; members of a school, church, or other organization are indeed conscious that their group's honor is implicated by their behavior. But no matter how much phenomena in our two societies bear empirical similarity, they are differentiated by contrasting backdrops of values about what social life *ought* to be. To take individual autonomy as the morally proper condition for an adult is to be firmly planted in the tradition of Western social ideals. To insist, rather, that one's personal conduct affects the larger collectivity, that one's life goals are not fully separable from one's family responsibilities, that marriage is not purely a private matter of the heart but a prerequisite to social respectability—and that respect in society is therefore not an automatic right of the individual—is to articulate a very different set of values indeed.

It was not until the fall of 1982 that I began a systematic study of those values. In the meantime I had married a Hirayama native, returned to America, and begun graduate work. My chosen field, anthropology, provided a reassuring perspective on my earlier experiences. "The Western conception of the person," writes one of its luminaries, "is, however incorrigible it may seem to us, a rather peculiar idea within the context of the world's cultures" (Geertz 1984: 126). The Japanese are hardly unique in possessing values that challenge our notion of the individual's place in society, of what it means to be a person.

My field also provided me with a strategy for the study that I came back to Hirayama to conduct. I had decided to investigate Japanese weddings, following a logic outlined by standard anthropological theory. Put simply, weddings are rites of passage; they belong to the class of rituals that everywhere mark the transition of an individual or group from one social status to another. Cross-culturally these rites have long been known to share a number of features. They typically contain ideal images of the social statuses about to be entered, for example, sometimes in the form of explicit verbalizations as found in wedding vows and speeches, sometimes as symbolic acts embodied in the ritual proceedings. Regardless of form, such images draw on shared values about the appropriate behavior for the statuses concerned. For weddings the statuses are, of course, those the principals will assume as married people, as husband and wife, but the relevance of these images extends much further. To say what it means to be a model husband and wife will engage more general ideals about relations between the sexes; such pronouncements may accordingly signal changing views of gender. Because the Japanese commonly view marriage as an entrance into adult society, moreover, statements of what it means to be a married person must also articulate views of the person's role as a member of society, and therefore touch on fundamental notions about society itself and the individual's place within it.

For all this, an important aspect of the material I would study fell outside standard anthropological experience. Japanese weddings have recently become thoroughly commercial affairs. Frequently held at home before the war, the vast majority are now conducted at establishments representing a specialized service industry, whose origin dates from the appearance of the wedding hall in the 1950s. This was the first commercial concern to combine facilities for a Shinto wedding ceremony and the ensuing reception under a single roof; it was soon joined by hotels and other institutions offering a similar range of services. The industry's rapid expansion is explained in part by its tactics of aggressive promotion. Prospective brides and grooms are enticed with images of romantic and sumptuous weddings appropriate for the celebration of their once-in-a-lifetime event. "A storybook ceremony of love," promises one wedding hall's brochure. "Your day of days, wrapped in the warm blessings of loved ones, in harmony and splendor." In bridal magazines advertisements for other establishments shout similar messages: "Joyful Wedding!" "Splendid Wedding!" "Colorful and Stylish!" "Paint Your Brightest Day Beautiful!"

How do these efforts to sell sumptuous and costly services affect the wedding's nature as a rite of passage? In what way might the presence of commercially defined goals distort the statements of values I was anticipating? The answers to such questions, I decided, required an examination of the wedding industry as a whole. The advantage of returning to Hirayama for my study became immediately apparent. Social networks already in place were enlisted, and soon after my arrival an introduction was arranged for me (through the auspices of a friend of my wife's family) with the personnel of White Crane Palace, the city's largest and oldest wedding hall.[1] There I talked with Nagai Masayuki, a pleasant man who oversees the service provided at the palace's wedding receptions. During the hour-long interview he answered my questions with enthusiasm, appearing genuinely delighted that I should take an interest in such matters. I was nevertheless nervous as I guided the conversation toward a plan I had recently formed. Given the seasonal nature of the business—weddings in Japan concentrate heavily in spring and fall—how did White Crane Palace cope with fluctuations in its requirements for manpower, I asked. As I had suspected, it relied on temporary help, including students hired on a daily basis. Would it be possible for me to perform such work?

Nagai hesitated briefly, then broke into a smile. "Let's give it a try."

For the next ten months I joined the White Crane Palace work force. On days when the wedding hall's schedule was busy, I labored long hours, helping prepare the ballrooms for receptions and cleaning up after the guests' departure. On slack days I was free to spend my time there in a more leisurely—and for my purposes more productive—fashion. Sometimes I donned a black waiter's suit and helped serve inside the ballroom during a reception. Sometimes I merely watched the proceedings from backstage or talked with the regular staff about their work. Sometimes I explored other divisions of the establishment, such as those in charge of sales and reservations. My experience there thus enabled close observation of wedding ritual,[2] my initial goal, while providing insights into the workings of the wedding industry as well.

There were other questions relating to contemporary weddings that also had to be examined as part of my study. Since my ultimate aim was to explore values that define what it means to be a person in Japanese society, I had to take account of recent discourse concerning those values. In prewar Japan the basic atom of society had clearly been not the individual but the *ie*, the domestic unit conceived as a hierarchically organized cooperative group under the authority of the household head, its representative to the wider society. Ideally the ie was a permanent entity, and the Meiji Civil Code of 1898 had in fact made its continuity a legal duty. The head of each generation was required to secure a successor in the next through birth, marriage, or if all else failed, adoption. He accordingly held authority over the marital choices of the ie's junior members—a fact that perhaps best illustrates the subordinate place accorded individual interests in prewar society.[3]

The Meiji Civil Code itself emerged only after a long debate focusing at the deepest levels on the very nature of society and the individual's position within it. A faction influential in the early years of the Meiji period (1868–1912) had in fact promoted the Western notion of individual autonomy as the basic principle of the social order. But the late nineteenth century saw a reaction against the direct emulation of Western customs, and the enactment of the Civil Code marked a major defeat for this faction.[4] The Meiji leaders chose instead a view of society more conducive to an ideology asserting the state's authority over the individual. Using the ie as their model, they expanded it to include the entire nation "based on the theory that Japan is a patriarchal state, all of whose people are related to one another and to the emperor, who is the supreme father" (Smith 1974: 26). The ie was thus seen as both society's minimal unit and its microcosmic representation, embodying the same underlying values of hierarchy and the individual's subordination to the larger group.

Japan's defeat in the Pacific War and the experiences immediately afterward fed expectations for significant changes in these values. One reason lay in the determination of American Occupation leaders to remold Japan into a Western-style democracy. The postwar Constitution they wrote accordingly provided an explicit guarantee of individual autonomy, necessitating the revision of the entire legal structure to incorporate this new principle. The revised Civil Code that went into effect in 1948 eliminated the ie as a legal entity, along with most of the prerogatives of the household head, and guaranteed people the right of free choice in marriage. The drafters of these reforms were conscious of the gap between explicitly formulated legal codes and more deeply rooted cultural values backed by the force of tradition, but they felt that legal mechanisms could help accelerate changes in values. They and many other Japanese believed, moreover, that urbanization and modernization were propelling Japanese society in more democratic directions in any case.

It seemed, then, that a general shift away from the traditional ie system and toward an individualistic orientation similar to that of the West was merely a matter of time, and observers of postwar society accordingly looked for indications of such a shift. Many focused specifically on the marriage process. The Japanese have traditionally distinguished between two types of marriage: those resulting from arranged introductions, called *miai kekkon*, and love matches, *ren'ai kekkon*, between people who meet on their own. An increase in the proportion of love matches was expected as more people began exercising the freedoms guaranteed by the new law, signaling acceptance of the new values. This assumption produced several sociological studies in the 1950s and 1960s.[5]

Would the ren'ai/miai dichotomy have the same meaning for my study? Would I find that weddings resulting from arranged introductions differ considerably from those resulting from love matches—suggesting they indeed reveal differences in values? And would the relative popularity of the two types of marriage thus serve as a basis for claiming that, despite the striking contrast in values I saw in my earlier experience, Western ideals are in fact gaining acceptance? These questions led me to conduct a series of interviews with married couples, in addition to my other research activities. I asked about their weddings and the events that had led up to them. I wanted to know, first of all, current attitudes toward the choice presented by love matches and arranged introductions, as well as whether this difference affects the kind of wedding held. But I was also interested in changes in wedding customs over the postwar period. Accordingly, I sought out people whose marriages dated from various times after the war, relying again on social networks I had built up in previous years. Some of the interviewees were old friends, others were people I met specifically for the purposes of this study.[6]

Since the main focus of this book is on the wedding as a window on Japanese values, I begin in the first chapter with a look at its modern form as observed at White Crane Palace. This description takes us into "the world of full-blown commercialization," which, a colleague has warned, is "not meant for the faint-hearted." Let me stress, however, that my aim is neither social criticism nor exposé; I wish merely to present an image of a socially meaningful performance that will command our attention until we can satisfactorily unravel its messages. Chapter 2 begins that task by providing historical background on the wedding and tracing the development of its modern form. I introduce the wedding's main actors, the bridal couple, in Chapter 3, which follows events involving them and their parents in both ren'ai and miai marriages up to the formalization of the engagement. Developments from that time until the wedding day are the subject of Chapter 4, which also takes a backstage look at the wedding hall and examines the role played by the personnel of the wedding industry. Chapter 5 begins an analysis of the symbolic content of the wedding by focusing on the image it projects of the ideal marital relationship. This analysis is pursued in Chapter 6, which examines how the marital ideal draws on values defining the most basic concepts of gender, person, and society. I conclude the work by looking briefly at the two historical issues raised in this Introduction: the relation of the wedding's commercialization to its symbolic content as a rite of passage, and the prospect that postwar values would ultimately converge toward Western individualism.

I follow the Japanese convention for personal names throughout, giving the surname first and given name last. The use of given names is limited to members of the Shimazaki family and, for convenience, to the informants whose marital histories are introduced in Chapters 3 and 4. All names are fictitious. In some instances I have taken the extra measure of changing details of age, family composition, and/or occupation to protect informants' identities.

Dollar equivalents in the text have been calculated at $1 = ¥240, the approximate rate of exchange during my fieldwork.

ONE

The Performance

The comment most often heard about the wedding nowadays is that it is "showy" (*hade*). While sometimes offered as criticism of its more commercial aspects, this term points nonetheless to a symbolic theme informing all of the wedding's proceedings. Other frequently used expressions amplify: "gay" or "colorful" (*hanayaka*); "splendid" and "gorgeous" (*gōka*). The day of the wedding is the couple's "brightest day," when they assume their "finest appearance"—especially the bride, who is said to be at her "most beautiful." These are more than just words to flatter the principals and their parents, who together stand as hosts for the wedding. They express the couple's proximity on this day to an ideal image of the marital relationship, an image the wedding as a performance portrays through its various activities. The performance is public, not simply because others are present, but because it draws on shared values concerning what it means to become husband and wife, and hence—as a married person—a full member of society. The examination of these values I leave for later chapters. Here I document the performance, as I observed it so often at White Crane Palace, which serves as a central arena for the articulation of those values in modern Japan.

The bride's part in the performance begins earliest. She must arrive at the wedding hall more than two hours before the others, since donning the traditional bridal kimono is a time-consuming process. The groom also comes early, although his preparations are completed much more quickly. He too begins the day in formal kimono, although until quite recently grooms wore Western-style suits throughout. Both need the assistance of wedding-hall employees in putting on the rented wedding clothes, so far removed from everyday life have these costumes become. Once dressed, the principals go to separate waiting rooms, where they are joined by their families and others who will accompany them during the Shinto ceremony. All told, these number perhaps twenty-five or thirty people.[1] Most are relatives—the principals' aunts, uncles, cousins, and grand-parents—but always included are a married couple who play a key role in the wedding, that of the *nakōdo*.

Although nakōdo is often translated as "go-between," the couple who fill this role may have had no hand in the making of the match. After the wedding, they are said to serve as guaran-tors for the marriage, taking an active interest in the principals' welfare and acting as conciliators should there be any serious marital dispute. They must appear in the wedding as an inter-ested party, therefore, and most commonly the nakōdo—the term normally refers to the husband only—turns out to be an older relative or a company superior of one of the principals, usually the groom. Other requirements signal the more funda-mental role the nakōdo plays at the wedding. He must be a mar-ried man and, more, one who has already demonstrated his ability to lead a stable married life. He is likely to be considerably older than the principals and ideally should be socially promi-nent and respected as well.

As a symbol of the successful union, then, the nakōdo con-tributes the dimension of social respectability to the image of the marital ideal being portrayed. The symbolic proximity of the principals to this ideal is expressed by their physical proximity to the living model: together with his wife, the nakōdo accom-panies the bride and groom throughout the ceremonies, sharing with them their place of honor separate from the rest of the wed-ding guests.[2] This spatial marking begins with the first part of the wedding, the Shinto ceremony.

The Shinto Ceremony

Although composed of elements rooted in Japan's ancient traditions, the Shinto ceremony has only recently become a standard part of the wedding. Accordingly, it is unfamiliar to most; the principals' parents, for example, are unlikely to have had a similar experience they can draw on as a model for their children. Moreover, wedding halls do not hold rehearsals for the ceremony as is common in church weddings in the West. Unfamiliarity with the proceedings often produces a vague tension among members of the wedding party. This is exacerbated by their uneasiness at having to interact with strangers, for many or most of the two groups of relatives are meeting each other for the first time, and under the most formal of circumstances.

The wedding hall deals with this tension by assembling the group for a meeting about twenty minutes before the ceremony. There an employee explains its content and what the couple must do, and soothes them with assurances that they will have no difficulty following the verbal instructions provided during the ceremony itself. At White Crane Palace this meeting is called the *taimenshiki* (literally, "meeting ceremony") because the employee also here introduces the bride's and groom's parties to one another by name. Designed to help break the ice for the two groups of relatives, it also gives the wedding hall better control over the flow of events to ensure a smooth performance, since on busy days the Shinto shrine is in continual use, with one party entering hard on the heels of another. Should the preceding party fall behind schedule, the introductions can be prolonged so the waiting group is not left to sit idle.

The shrine is contained in a single room, used only for wedding ceremonies and otherwise kept closed. It is of course no older than the wedding hall but, by the logic governing such matters, it embodies ancient Shinto traditions as a subbranch of a branch of one of the oldest and most famous of Japanese shrines, to whose deity it is dedicated. Its claim to authenticity is reinforced by the beat of a large drum and music from a traditional style of flute, both characteristic of Shinto ceremony, played through overhead speakers as the party enters. At the far end of the room stands the altar; near it sit two priests and two young women dressed as *miko* (shrine maidens).[3] Once inside, the couple and the nakōdo and his wife separate from the rest and sit at two small tables in the center of the room, the couple in front. Members of the groom's party take places at a long table to their right, his parents nearest the altar. The bride's party occupies a table to the left in similar fashion.

The ceremony consists of practices shared with other Shinto

rituals (purification, prayer, invocation, and offering) mixed with customs whose presence makes it distinctly a wedding (the ring exchange, the recitation of wedding vows, and the sharing of *sake* cups). An employee of the wedding hall directs the proceedings from the back of the room by announcing upcoming events and giving verbal instructions to the participants. The shrine maidens' stylized movements similarly serve to prompt action at appropriate points. The concern of all to avoid miscues is no doubt heightened by the presence of two video cameras, suspended from the ceiling to the right and left of the altar. They are manipulated by a technician in an adjacent room, who alternately zooms in on the couple or other key actors and pans the faces of the relatives along the side wall, as he makes a videotape of the proceedings for the couple to keep. The cameras also remind the participants of the larger audience outside the room. Guests invited only for the reception have already begun to gather in the wedding hall's lobby, where the ceremony is shown on a large monitor for their benefit.

The employee begins the ceremony with a statement of its purpose: to solemnly unite the man and woman before the *kami* (deity) through the auspices of the nakōdo. He instructs all present to stand and bow toward the altar. One of the priests utters a short prayer, then picks up an instrument for purification (*harai-gushi*), a long stick with a great number of strips of white paper attached to one end. Jerking this quickly left, right, and left, he produces a loud "Whoosh! Whoosh! Whoosh!" to purify the room and its participants. The priest then chants an invocation (*norito*). Although, like the prayer, it uses arcane language fully comprehensible only to those who have received special training, its gist is clear enough. The participants listen respectfully while the priest addresses several deities (including Izanagi and Izanami, the primal couple credited in myth with procreating the universe), proclaims the bride and groom united through the auspices of the nakōdo, and prays for the happiness and prosperity of the match.

The employee then announces the first of three *sakazukigoto*, the ritual sharing of *sake* that creates or reinforces social bonds. The second priest begins an accompaniment of high-pitched, wailing notes on a wooden flute. With quick, precise movements, the miko bring a vessel filled with *sake* and a tray holding three nested cups to the principals' table. One miko extends the tray for the groom to take the topmost cup, the other then pours a small amount of *sake*, which he drinks with a series of three sipping motions. He returns the cup and the tray is offered to the bride who drinks (or pretends to drink) from the same cup in similar fashion. This procedure is repeated with the second and third cups. Each of the principals thus sips three times from all three cups, and many popular etiquette books (e.g. Iida and Fujioka 1979: 87) offer this as the reason for the ceremony's common name, *san-san-ku-do* ("three, three, nine times").[4]

The flute music starts up again as the bride drinks from the last of the three cups. The miko then serve *sake* from it to (in order) the groom's father, the groom's mother, the groom, the bride's father, and the bride's mother. Finally the two groups of relatives share *sake*, together with the nakōdo. Once the miko have poured *sake* into the small cups set on the tables for each person, the employee instructs everyone to pick them up and cues the assemblage to drink together by proclaiming "*Omedetō gozaimasu*" ("Congratulations").

At the employee's instructions, the groom picks up a text from the table in front of him and reads the wedding vows:

> We have now become united as husband and wife for all ages before the *kami* at White Crane Palace. We respectfully pledge from here on to make our hearts as one, give mutual help and support, faithfully execute our marital duties and responsibilities, and spend all the days of our lives together with unchanging trust and eternal affection.

He closes by reading the date and his full name; the bride adds her first name only.

The couple then make a traditional offering of *tamagushi* to the kami—strips of white paper attached to branches of the sacred *sakaki* tree. The miko bring the bride and groom these items and lead them to the altar, where each presents the branch in the prescribed manner by turning its base first toward the body, then toward the altar, before laying it down. Everyone in the hall joins in at the end with two bows, two hand-claps, and another bow, cued verbally by the employee and visually by the exaggerated movements of the miko, who perform these acts while standing on either side of the couple before the altar.

The couple return to their places for the ring exchange. A miko brings the box holding the rings and extends it to the groom for him to take the bride's ring, which he places on her finger. As the bride completes the exchange, the employee prompts the audience to applaud. The other miko now advances with a set of items White Crane Palace presents to all couples who get married in its shrine. This includes an album for keeping wedding memorabilia and an amulet from the hall's famous parent shrine. The formalities close with everyone making a final bow toward the altar. The priest who performed the invocation faces the group and announces the successful completion of the ceremony, offering his congratulations to all and instructing the newlyweds to build a harmonious home.

Doors along a side wall open to an adjoining photographic studio. The entire party enters for the first pose, a group shot along with the guests in the lobby. Afterward the bride and groom remain for several more poses. The nakōdo and his wife stay with them while the others proceed to the ballroom for the reception. They are greeted at the door by waitresses in kimono, who hand them seating charts so they can find their places inside.

The Reception: Formality

The reception opens with a series of formal events: the newly-weds' entrance, speeches by the nakōdo and the most important guests, and then several ritual acts, which usually include the cutting of the wedding cake and always end with a toast (*kanpai*). This part of the reception is the time of greatest sustained focus on the wedding's portrayal of the marital ideal, and also of greatest concern for the wedding hall about the event's success. But in contrast to the Shinto ceremony, which follows a highly standardized script acted mostly by the wedding hall's own personnel, the hall's personnel are here limited to the indirect roles of cueing, prompting, setting the stage, providing the props. The responsibility for these functions falls primarily to a single employee I refer to as the director.

As soon as the photo session is over, the director leads the couple and the nakōdo and his wife to the ballroom, to stand poised before the now-closed double doors. Inside the guests wait expectantly. The person who serves as emcee—usually a friend of the groom—stands at a podium near the entrance. When all is ready, the director signals the emcee, who announces the entrance and calls for the guests' applause. An assistant to the director, usually one of the more experienced waitresses, dims the lights and starts a tape recording of music the principals have previously selected, usually Mendelssohn's "Wedding March." The assistant will also shine a spotlight on the newlyweds as they make their way to their table at the far end of the room.

The director enters first, followed at a distance of several paces by the nakōdo and then the groom. The nakōdo's wife comes next, steadying the bride, who is burdened by the traditional bridal costume with its heavy, constricting robes, precarious wig, and headdress. The director walks very slowly, one step per bar of the score, taking a full minute to lead the group from the entrance down the long aisle between the guests' tables. Experience tells him that if left to themselves, the members of the group might cover this distance in a fraction of the time, losing a precious opportunity to project a dignified and dramatic image. As the two couples reach their table, which rests on a platform several inches above floor level, the director steps quickly aside, motioning them to mount and take their places. The assistant brings up the lights, and the group now stands in full view of the guests. Applause swells at the emcee's prompting. The couples hold their pose while guests with cameras come forward and take their picture. Finally the music stops, the applause dies down, and the director signals the group to sit.

The Opening Speeches

The emcee now introduces himself to the guests and offers his congratulations to the newlyweds and their families. Often he prefaces these remarks in the same way that Japanese typically open a letter—with a poetic reference to the weather or the changing seasons—one of several conventions formal speech borrows from the realm of written language. He then introduces the nakōdo, who gives the first of the opening speeches. The director motions the party at the principals' table to stand and hands the nakōdo a microphone. His assistant, meanwhile, instructs the couple's parents to stand at their places at the other end of the room.

The nakōdo's speech follows a standard format. Ostensibly its purpose is to introduce the bride and groom to the guests, who normally are acquainted with only one or the other of them. But in performing this task the nakōdo also reinforces the wedding's symbolic message, for his introduction stresses the couple's closeness to commonly held ideals. They are well brought up and educated, he claims, responsible workers and active individuals, the kind of young man or woman any parent would gladly have his child wed. The following text exemplifies these themes.

I sincerely thank all of you for taking time from your busy schedules to come today. It gives me great pleasure to announce the successful completion of the wedding ceremony of the Uchiyama and Okamoto families on this auspicious day, in solemn and decorous fashion before the *kami*. There are no words for the happiness of the bride and groom on this day, a happiness I am certain is shared by their parents, brothers and sisters, and other relatives. It is a great privilege and a pleasure for me to fill the important role of *nakōdo* for the couple's marriage.

No doubt many who have come to this reception today to offer words of congratulations to the bride and groom are already familiar with their backgrounds and personalities. It is my hope, however, that by demonstrating how truly ideal this marriage is, how suitable the principals are for each other, and how their personalities are naturally and mutually compatible, I can share with you anew a sincere and heartfelt joy for the couple.

The groom, Takao, was born on the twenty-first of June, 1954, as the second of three children, all of them boys, in the Uchiyama family. He spent his childhood growing up in fortunate circumstances, entering Moriyama Elementary School in 1961, East Hirayama Junior High School in 1967, and East Hirayama Senior High School in 1970. In 1973 he went to Tokyo to study in the Faculty of Law at Kantō University. An accomplished scholar-athlete, he competed on his university's judo team, a sport he took up in junior high, while compiling an outstanding academic record. After graduating in 1977, he returned to Hirayama and overcame fierce competition to enter the municipal civil service, scoring exceptionally high on the entrance exam in a year when the ratio of applicants to the number of openings was over thirty to one.

He has since worked at City Hall in the Public Health and Revenue departments, and for the past four years has been working with me in the Department of Motor Vehicles. He always conducts himself on the job with responsibility and adheres strictly to regulations. He is recognized by all as a young man of outstanding character with a bright and promising future. I am fond of thinking of him as an ideal worker and a model for others: one who actively pursues his own thinking and ideas most thoroughly, but who is also willing to follow the lead of superiors. The groom remains active in sports and is a key member of a team in the Upper Division of the Municipal Softball League. He also participates in a variety of sporting events organized among the workers at City Hall, including tennis, basketball, and baseball.

The bride, Setsuko, was born on the seventh of January, 1956, as the eldest child of the Okamoto family. She has two siblings, a brother and a sister. Her father is an educator who is currently the principal of an elementary school. . . .

After giving the bride's educational history and praising her academic and athletic accomplishments as he did in introducing the groom, the nakōdo continues:

After junior college Setsuko began working at City Hall in the Department of Motor Vehicles. She is a very healthy and cheerful person with a wonderful personality, and a very hard worker. What's more, she is, as you can all plainly see, extremely beautiful. Our department was instantly brightened by her presence. After working in several other departments in City Hall, she was employed for more than two years in the office of an accounting firm.

The couple started seeing each other from the time Takao came to work at City Hall over four years ago. They decided to marry late last spring and were formally engaged in June.

The bride and groom, as I have already said, are extremely well suited for each other. They can truly be called a perfect couple. But because they are still young and lacking in experience, I would like to close these remarks by asking you all to give them more of your kind guidance and encouragement in the future.[5]

As the guests applaud the nakōdo's speech, the director signals the parties at the principals' and parents' tables to take their seats. The emcee then introduces the first *shuhin* ("principal guest"), a person who will speak as a representative of those invited to the reception. Two or more people may speak in this capacity, always alternating between a guest on the groom's side and one on the bride's. Usually they are the couple's current or past company superiors, but others, such as former teachers, may also be asked to fill this role. As the emcee introduces each shuhin, the director escorts him from his seat to one of the microphones standing on either side of the newlyweds' table.

Many speakers come prepared with notes; some have the entire text written out. Often their speeches echo the nakōdo's by offering praise for the couple's character, capabilities, and interests. However, they frequently add another dimension to the image of the principals as approaching the marital ideal by setting out moral lessons for the couple in their life ahead or expressing high expectations for their future achievements. The following example, delivered by a groom's company superior, is also typical in beginning with an expression of deference at being asked to speak before others.

Although it is not my place to do so, I have been called upon to speak, so I would like to say a few words appropriate to this happy occasion. Neither am I accustomed to speaking in such formal circumstances, so I will simply speak in my usual manner.

[To the bride and groom:] Mr. Hayashi, Noriko, congratulations on your marriage. I am certain that the parents who have raised you to this day are too happy for words.

As the *nakōdo* has already explained, it is now over five years since the groom came to work in our company. In that time he has earned the confidence of both his fellow workers and our customers and has become a very responsible and capable worker. We have great hopes for him in the future, so I ask everyone for guidance and support on his behalf. . . .

For a couple to truly love each other and build a good home it is best that they have common goals and ideals regarding work and life-styles, and work together to achieve their goals. I believe this is the basis of an ideal marriage. I hope the bride and groom work toward their common goals and build a happy home based on mutual understanding and faith.

Speakers often add warnings about difficulties ahead for the couple in their new life. Some offer concrete reasons for marital trouble: "Since the two have grown up in completely different surroundings, there will be differences between them in many things . . . even their tastes in soup." Others prefer indirection, resorting to metaphoric terms: "It seems that many things in life are beyond our comprehension. I'm sure there are times of joy ahead as well as times when you will wonder why life is so painful. Today's wedding is the emergence of a new flower. The future will bring both warm winds to make it bloom and cold winds that cut at the roots." Many advise couples to meet such times by recalling the experience of the wedding day itself. "Do not forget this feeling today, when you are able to receive the best wishes of all these people," urged a groom's former teacher. The boss of another groom, warning of "dark and difficult times" ahead, added: "Please do not forget the deep feeling of today in such times and, taking each other's hand, build a warm and pleasant household."

The guests listen politely throughout the fifteen minutes or more it takes for the nakōdo and shuhin to finish speaking. Most, however, find these speeches boring, and for good reason: it is commonly held ideals that are projected; speakers rarely say anything the listeners have not heard before. Younger people especially are more interested in the celebrations they know will begin shortly. But they must wait a bit longer, until the completion of one of the wedding's richest symbolic acts—the cutting of the wedding cake—an event that draws deeply on the director's stage-managing skills to develop still further the central image of the marital ideal.

The Cake-Cutting Ceremony

The emcee begins the cake-cutting—as he does all other events—with an introduction, a role the wedding hall considers so important for a successful performance that it provides him with a script beforehand. If he follows this verbatim, he will signal one of the themes of the cake-cutting by announcing it as "the first step of cooperation in the couple's new life." Many emcees who write their own scripts express similar sentiments. One invited the couple "to give us a demonstration of marital harmony by together inserting the knife into the cake."[6] All are careful to invite guests with cameras to come forward and get ready.

Outwardly, the cake looks no different from that used in our wedding ceremonies. It is the white bride's cake in its most elaborate form, with three or sometimes four tiers and nearly four feet high, topped by miniature figures of a bridal couple in Western dress. Long red and white ribbons stream from their feet down to the base of the cake. There is a vast difference, however: the Japanese cake is inedible. The frosting, with its carefully sculpted swirls, ribbons, and rose blossoms, is usually made of hard wax, or more recently, of molded rubber. A small slot in back receives the blunt blade of the knife, which like the cake itself is merely a prop in an elaborately staged event. The cake rests on a cylindrical stand about three feet tall that also plays a part in this production, as we shall shortly see.

During the emcee's announcement, the director leads the couple from their table to the cake standing prominently to one side. His assistant dims the lights, shines a spotlight on them, and starts a tape of music they have selected to accompany the event. Most couples choose one of the songs White Crane Palace offers as standard choices. Many also elect to have the tape dubbed with a woman's voice reciting a poetic expression of the bride's feelings as she stands ready to cut the cake with the groom. Like the music, the poem is highly sentimental:

> I know,
> It is only because of you
> That here I stand.
>
> I know,
> Because you smile, I too
> Beam and nod my head.
>
> You have taught me love's true treasure.
> Now, our hands together poised above our wedding cake . . .
> Take this hand gently, firmly.
> Lead it always, and forever I will follow.
>
> Now, my heart is filled
> With the joy of loving you.

Some couples produce a substitute text of their own, an arrangement the wedding hall prefers because it makes a more memorable impression. This may be a tape the bride dubbed before the wedding or a piece that is read by one of her friends. Such texts usually resemble the wedding hall's version, expanding on the theme of togetherness set out in the emcee's introduction:

> In you I have found my one and only. As poor as I am at opening myself to others, I am able to open up to you. As selfish as I am, I have become more selfish and dependent on you.

Although there have been sad and difficult moments this past year, let us forget these and steadily tread the path to happiness together. Tying [*kakete*] a ribbon around my many memories of the past, and holding [*kakete*] high hopes for our future together, I step forth hand in hand to be with the one I love. Thus today my dreams come true, as I go to be your wife.

During the narration the director takes the knife, the blade carefully wrapped in a linen napkin, and places the handle in the groom's hands, on which the bride lightly rests hers. Keeping the blade covered with the napkin, the director positions the tip in the slot in back of the cake. At the end of the narration, he pulls off the napkin and brings it high over his head in one sweeping motion while stepping quickly backward. This is the cue for the emcee to announce the moment in a loud voice, prompting the guests to applaud. As the director steps back he turns a switch releasing hot water onto a piece of dry ice concealed inside the cylindrical cake stand, causing a thick cloud of vapor to envelop the cake's base as the emcee makes his announcement. The bride and groom remain standing, sometimes frozen and sometimes managing a smile, with vapor flowing, cameras flashing, guests applauding, and the music continuing to play for a full minute. During this interval the guests' interest may flag, forcing the emcee to take up the slack with a request for another round of applause or a hyperbolic comment about the couple's appearance ("The most splendid couple in all Japan!"). Despite this risk the tape is timed to run the extra minute or more to give those with cameras ample opportunity for taking pictures, and because drawing out the moment into a pose is felt to make the event more memorable.

As the music ends the director removes the knife from the cake, again carefully covering the blade with the napkin, and escorts the couple back to their places. The emcee then announces the kanpai and asks the guests to rise. The man designated to lead the toast, usually an older relative of the groom's or one of his company superiors, goes to one of the microphones at the front of the room. With a few brief remarks he toasts the happiness of the couple and their families, ending with a sharp "*Kanpai!*," which the guests echo as they all raise their cups to their lips in unison.

The Reception: Informality

The kanpai is followed by more speeches, interspersed with events as carefully staged by the wedding hall as the cake-cutting. But the kanpai also marks the start of the banquet, during which the guests can eat, drink, relax, and talk through whatever proceedings are going on. Indeed at times this informal feasting is the only activity. But what may look like people merely having a good time has another dimension, one that gives it a serious, almost obligatory nature. Weddings do more than create a social bond between two individuals. They create ties, however tenuous, between groups of kith and kin as well. The solidarity being established between husband and wife must be similarly enacted by the guests—not doing so would make the wedding a failure.

At all Japanese banquets alcohol is a key instrument in promoting such solidarity, since drinking is by necessity a social activity. Etiquette forbids a person from filling his own cup, forcing participants to alternate between the roles of provider and beneficiary of the hospitable act of serving. These exchanges take place between people sitting adjacent to or opposite one another, for example, as part of the normal course of carrying on conversation. Serving is also important as a pretext for social interaction with those seated farther away. During the informal part of the reception, many of the guests can be seen leaving their seats, bottle in hand, to go and offer a drink to someone as a means of starting a conversation. The couple's parents are especially likely to go around the room in this manner, greeting the guests and pausing for the obligatory cup forced on them in return. Such socializing continues until the reception's closing moments, sometimes accompanying and sometimes alternating with activities more expressive in nature. But even these activities have a more relaxed character to them, and they grow increasingly less formal as the wedding wears on.

The change from the formal to the informal part of the reception is explicitly marked by the bride's change of dress. Shortly after the kanpai, the emcee announces that the bride is leaving for her first *ironaoshi* (from *iro*, "color," plus *naosu*, "to change, correct"), a change of clothes traditionally used to symbolize the transition to married status. The bride is accompanied from the ballroom by the nakōdo's wife. When she returns twenty-five minutes later, she will have changed from the traditional bridal robe into a *furisode*, a formal kimono worn by young women until marriage.

Her return entrance offers still other opportunities for a symbolic emphasis on the marital ideal. Usually the groom is summoned to join her, so that at the emcee's announcement the doors open to reveal the couple standing together, the groom to the bride's right. Over their heads he holds a paper umbrella, a traditional symbol of lovers when shared by a man and a woman. As they make their way to their table to the accompaniment of applause, the emcee comments on this image of togetherness and asks the couple to hold their pose until the guests have finished taking snapshots. Sometimes the imagery is further embellished by having the bride enter with her father, who holds the umbrella. The groom meets them halfway down the aisle, taking both the umbrella and the bride from her father in an exchange the emcee describes as "passing the baton" (*baton tatchi*).

Congratulatory Speeches

A series of congratulatory speeches (*shukuji*) begins shortly after the kanpai and continues until the closing moments of the reception, interspersed with other activities and periods of feasting. First to speak are the more important guests after the shuhin—company superiors, former teachers, or older relatives of the principals. These speakers usually enlarge on the ideals voiced by earlier ones. Many emphasize that marriage brings a new role in society, one that is much more demanding. "With today's start the couple's responsibilities in society will become much greater," declared one person, adding that "people will also look at them in a different light." Another speaker explained: "The bride and groom are today taking their first steps as members of society. Until now no one has recognized them as such, but as of today everyone should treat them as fully adult." As adults, however, they must "work to repay to society the debt [*on*] they have incurred from the parents who raised them until now." The Japanese have long used the concept of *on*—a moral debt one can never discharge—to express the demands society places on the individual. Other speakers use different expressions, but the image of society as difficult and demanding remains the same. The uncle of one groom stated it metaphorically: "Together you must now sail forth into society's rough waves. I hope you do your best to hold a steady course. There will be times when the going is difficult, so you will have to set your hearts firmly."

Later on, the emphasis of the speeches shifts. Younger guests—friends of the bride and groom—speak less formally, often simply telling anecdotes about experiences shared with one of the principals. Much to the amusement of all, these frequently contain embarrassing revelations of the principals' past misconduct, as if to serve as a reminder of their fallibility as humans in face of the ideals being projected. One speaker tells of sneaking into a pornographic movie with the groom when they were in junior high school. Another mixes words of praise with hints about past romantic involvements:

Congratulations, Takeshi, on your marriage.

As the emcee just said, the groom and I have been friends from childhood. We lived in the same neighborhood, went to the same elementary and junior high schools, and now work for the same company, so I can say I know him very well. I also know people are apt to think he is very cool and reserved, judging just from his looks, but at heart he is really a very warm, gentle, and considerate person. . . . I'm sure these qualities will help him in his married life.

But he also likes to fool around [*asobi*] well enough.[7] He likes to go drinking a lot and [pause] well, I was warned beforehand not to say anything about his past love life, but suffice it to say he is a very sociable person who is certain to continue to get along well with his fellows and superiors at our company, in addition to leading a harmonious life at home. I'd like to ask all here to give him your cooperation in the future. Thank you.

Some speakers play counterpoint to the wedding's ideals with puns, parodies, and an occasional ribald joke. Women speakers refrain from anything risque, but may make ample use of other means of lightening the tone of an otherwise laudatory speech:

Congratulations to the couple, their families and relatives. As the emcee just explained, I have been a friend of the bride's since high school, where [we] were very close, always going everywhere together. We were so inseparable that people thought there must be something strange about us, so you can see why I feel today as though something is being taken away from me. But if she is able to get along with the groom and stay with him, and since both have Type A blood I suppose it is all right [a pun: the speaker uses the colloquial form *ee*, meaning "all right," and pronounced like the letter A]. I hope they work hard toward having a good married life.

I have brought something I would like to present to the groom on behalf of the bride's friends. [The speaker reads the following text parodying the language of modern marketing.]

PRODUCT WARRANTY

We certify this product to be, regardless of her looks, endowed with superior health, discretion, and common sense, outstanding qualities of perseverance and enthusiasm, and an extremely considerate disposition. She is, moreover, amazingly sensitive, observant, and receptive, despite all appearances to the contrary. Granted that every human fault is not without its compensations, we feel she is a completely satisfactory product.

We therefore guarantee that with careful and gentle handling and generous amounts of love she will maintain her original charm and give long years of faithful and dedicated service. The purchaser is warned, however, that under no circumstances can this product be returned, so he is advised to exercise proper care and caution.

Because of such lighthearted elements, shukuji blend in easily with the singing and other performances by the guests in the latter part of the reception. Mixed with these, however, is another performance that directly involves the bride and groom, one carefully engineered by the wedding hall to develop further the wedding's image of the marital ideal.

The Candle Service

About thirty minutes after the bride's second entrance, she is led out by the nakōdo's wife for yet another change of clothes. The groom leaves alone, also to change, several minutes later. When they return, the director signals the emcee to announce the candle service. Again the lights dim, music begins to play, and a spotlight follows the couple as they enter to the guests' applause. Both are now in formal Western dress, and each holds a long, unlit candle. Following the director, the couple goes first to the table of the groom's parents, on which a candle stands already lit. The groom lights his candle from his parents' candle, and the two proceed to the bride's parents' table. There the bride lights her candle in similar fashion. The director then leads the couple around the room, stopping at the one or two floral arrangements placed on every table, each of which holds a single unlit candle, to which the bride and groom simultaneously touch their flames. As the newlyweds light each candle in turn, the guests seated nearby greet them with cheers and applause. Their response may be prompted by the emcee, but the enthusiasm is often genuinely spontaneous. If the reception has become sufficiently merry, for example, the groom's friends are likely to use this moment as further opportunity to tease him by wetting the wick of the candle in front of them. They then take great delight in his difficulty as he attempts to light it, shouting at him to get on with it and cheering heartily when the candle is finally lit.

Proceeding to their own table, the couple light the candles that stand in front of the nakōdo and his wife, while the emcee expresses thanks to them on the newlyweds' behalf and asks the nakōdo to continue guiding them in the future. The bride and groom now stand at their places and face the guests. In the center of the table before them stands a single two-foot-high candle. The emcee again gives guests with cameras ample time to position themselves, then instructs the couple to light the candle as he narrates: "Now the moment comes for the lighting of the Wedding Candle. The separate flames of love and life that the bride and groom received from their parents who have raised them until this day are united to form the couple's new life. Please nurture this flame to make it endure and burn brightly." The guests applaud while the couple remain posed behind the lit candle for still more photographs, before finally sitting down.

Entertainments

After the candle service, congratulatory speeches give way increasingly to various kinds of entertainments. Some guests combine the two by giving a short speech and then a performance; others opt for the performance alone. Those who have studied traditional forms of dance, for example, or can play a musical instrument or recite bits of classical literature may come prepared to show their skills. These have always been popular at Japanese banquets, and are often performed by the older guests. Younger guests are more likely to sing, and rely increasingly on *karaoke*, jukebox-like machines that play the accompaniment to popular songs to which they sing the lyrics. Almost half of White Crane Palace's customers now rent karaoke, stocked with tunes that are perennial favorites at weddings as well as with the latest romantic hits. Less often, clients rent a piano or electric organ on which one of the guests, or in some cases a professional hired through the wedding hall, provides live accompaniment.

Another common form of entertainment consists of the guests' attempts to tease the newlyweds, especially the groom, into revealing some intimate detail of their relationship or making a public display of affection. Like earlier congratulatory speeches, this teasing plays on the contrast between the publicly projected ideal and what it masks or leaves out. In this case it is the more romantic and even sexual aspects of a relationship otherwise soberly portrayed as a matter of domestic harmony and social duty. The simplest form is a short "interview," often conducted by the emcee, in which the bride and groom stand up and are asked, separately or together, a series of stock questions: what was your first impression of the bride (groom)? when (or where) did you first kiss? how did the groom propose? how many children do you want? The question-and-answer session is usually followed by a demand that the bride and groom kiss. Although kissing in public is rare in Japan, the guests urge the couple on, and the groom responds by giving the (usually) reticent bride a peck on the cheek as she turns her face away, to the combined cheers and laughter of those watching.

The Flower Presentation and the Closing Speeches

Entertainments do not continue much beyond the candle service—the newlyweds usually must catch a train to begin their honeymoon, and most of the guests are restless and ready to head for home. A series of events soon follows that brings the reception to its emotional climax and then its close. The series

begins with the flower presentation, the last of the wedding
hall's carefully staged events.

The emcee begins the presentation by announcing it as an expression of the couple's gratitude to their parents for having
raised them until their wedding day. The bride and groom stand
to the side of their table in full view of the guests, each holding a
bouquet of flowers and a carnation. Their parents also stand,
facing them from the opposite end of the room. The lights dim
and a tape begins to play. This music, as before, is typically selected from tapes offered by White Crane Palace, though the
couple may opt to provide a tape of their own. Usually there is
some form of narration as well. This may be a standard text or
something written by the couple, dubbed onto the tape or read
by a friend. The voice is normally that of a woman, although the
content does not necessarily express only the bride's point of
view. Standard texts often attempt to create a feel for the details
of the principals' upbringing. The following example refers to
the joy that attended the speaker's birth.

How impatiently Father must have waited the time I was born. How
happy Mother must have been when I was born. How did my face
look? How did my voice sound? Peering at me over and again, Father
suddenly shouts for joy; Mother holds me tightly to her breast.

Although my newborn eyes could not see it, now it is clear. I see the
white in Father's hair; I see the wrinkles multiply on Mother's hands.

Even though we too are soon to become mother and father ourselves,
whenever I look to the sky I see Father's cloud; wherever I walk Mother's
shadow follows behind.[8]

At the end of the narration a spotlight follows the couple as they
walk across the room to where their parents stand waiting. At
the director's signal they stop and bow, each in front of the
other's parents. They then step forward and together present
the floral bouquets to the (other's) mother, and insert the carnation in the father's lapel.

The emcee may prompt applause during the presentation if
necessary, but ordinarily applause and emotion pour forth spon-
taneously. The guests have already been put in a highly sentimental mood; even the rowdiest of revelers is gradually calmed
by the music and the narration, and by the sight of the newlyweds standing with heads bowed, choked with emotion, the

bride raising her handkerchief from time to time to wipe away a tear. As the couple passes among the guests, applause starts and swells to a peak during the presentation. Many of the guests are also moved to tears, especially the bride's friends. The parents are even more likely to be overcome with emotion.

After the presentation, the director lines the newlyweds up between their parents, all facing the guests together. The emcee now announces that the reception is drawing to a close and introduces two final speakers. The first is the groom's father (or a surrogate), who thanks the guests as a representative of the pair's parents; he is followed by the groom, speaking for himself and his bride. Both speeches are short and similar in content. The groom's father always begins with words of thanks and ends with a request for future support for the couple:

> I would like to say a word of gratitude on behalf of the Tabata and Ishino families.
> I wish to thank you all from the bottom of my heart for coming today in the midst of your busy schedules, and some of you from so far away.
> The *nakōdo*, the *shuhin*, various friends and relatives, have all given the bride and groom warm words of guidance and encouragement. I am sure these words will be engraved in their hearts as they start their new life together. Thank you very much.
> As you can see, the couple is still very young and inexperienced. I sincerely ask all of you here today to continue giving them your guidance and support in the future, and I pray you will keep kind watch over their further development.
> Thanking you once again for all you have done today, I close these simple greetings on behalf of the two families.

The groom's speech is even shorter. He gives a reduced version of the thoughts just expressed by his father, to which he may add a pledge to try to live up to the ideals of married life set out by earlier speakers:

> We wish to thank you very much for coming today and making this reception such a splendid event for us.
> We hope in the future to build a bright and harmonious home life. Since we are still immature, we ask your future guidance.
> Thank you very much.

As the applause dies down, the director leads the couple's parents back to their seats. The bride and groom remain standing; the emcee asks everyone to rise for a group cheer (*banzai*). This is usually led by one of the relatives, who briefly dedicates the event to the couple's future happiness and the prosperity of the two families. He then shouts "Banzai!" while quickly raising both arms over his head, hands apart with palms facing forward. Once the rest of the group has performed the same shout and gesture in response, the leader drops his arms and repeats it a second, then a third time.

At this point the emcee may briefly announce the couple's honeymoon plans or their new place of residence. Otherwise, he simply declares the reception over and thanks the guests for their participation, apologizing for his inadequate performance. He instructs the bride and groom to take their leave by going first to thank the nakōdo and his wife, and asks the guests to send them off with generous applause. The director leads the couple through the aisles while his assistant starts the final tape, usually an upbeat selection that soon has the guests clapping to the rhythm. As they pass among the guests, the bride and groom receive applause, smiles, expressions of good wishes, and many congratulatory handshakes and pats on the shoulder. They may become very emotional, especially when they reach their families' tables, where one of them often breaks down and cries uncontrollably for several moments. Following the director, they finally make their way back to the entrance, turn once again to face the guests, bow, and leave. They are soon joined outside the door by their parents, along with the nakōdo and his wife. The guests, meanwhile, pack up the items they are to take home—gifts from the hosts (*hikidemono*) and any untouched food from the banquet packed into a small cardboard box—and bid farewell to the group lined up outside the door as they exit.

Many guests return home directly from the wedding hall. Others, mostly contemporaries of the newlyweds, go to the station to await their arrival and see them off on their honeymoon. In the meantime, the bride and groom change and pick up their travel gear before leaving for the station, some six hours or more after their arrival at the wedding hall.

Background

"Of course, we did none of this sort of thing in my day."

Mrs. Shibata, one of the waitresses at White Crane Palace, spoke in reference to a wedding like the one described in Chapter 1. I was helping her clean the ballroom afterward—part of my job at the wedding hall—when the conversation took place.

Often the pace of work permitted no conversation at all. On busy days a ballroom is used two or even three times in succession, leaving a scant hour in between to clean up after one reception and prepare for the next. Even less time is available should the preceding wedding lag behind schedule. Personnel from the business office may be enlisted to assist the waitresses and student helpers on such occasions; it is not uncommon to see the company's managing director, a portly man in his sixties, frantically busing dirty dishes alongside a high school youth. One step behind them a waitress wipes the table surface clean, while others rearrange chairs or bring in the dishes to be set out for each guest. The head waitress and the man who is to serve as director dash about barking orders to the group.

"Set out twelve chairs on this row! Fourteen on that side and eleven over here!"

"It's the thirteen-piece course this time! Leave room for the tempura to the left of the main dish!"

"No time to put the *hikidemono* on the chairs—bring them out at the end of the reception!"

A far more leisurely mood prevails in the ballroom after the final reception of the day. With no more deadlines to meet, there is time to relax and engage in small talk during the cleanup, and time for me to ask about things I had observed during the day. There is also time to pick up gossip about deviations from the wedding's ideal pattern. One groom cried so much he was unable to finish his speech. That bride last week was surely pregnant already—that's why her family acted so coolly toward the groom. Another bride wore Western clothes throughout—not because of a pregnancy, a good reason for avoiding the tight obi of the bridal kimono, but simply because the high wig that goes with it would have made her look taller than the groom, or so she claimed.

It was during one such conversation that Mrs. Shibata contrasted the day's events with her own wedding some thirty years before. She and her husband had also had a Shinto ceremony—performed, however, at an independent shrine, Hirayama's largest, rather than inside a commercial facility like White Crane Palace. The kimono she wore was of the furisode style, rented from a local beautician, both simpler and less costly than the *uchikake* worn today. Afterward they held a reception at a nearby restaurant, one that differed little from other old-fashioned banquets. People sat on tatami mats, there was no emcee, although the nakōdo performed some of this role by giving the opening greetings, and the restaurant neither recommended a format for the proceedings nor oversaw its performance in the manner of the contemporary wedding hall director. In fact, Mrs. Shibata claimed, there was hardly any format at all. "It was one long party—all we did was drink."

Other descriptions from early postwar years confirm this image of simplicity in both wedding and reception. Many of the subsequent changes are the work of commercial institutions like White Crane Palace, which have introduced such events as the wedding cake, the candle service, and the flower presentation. I will later argue that the general acceptance of these and other recent innovations has depended on their ability to articulate values appropriate to the context—values concerning the nature of the marital bond, the proper shape of relations between husbands and wives, and the role of the individual, as a married person, in the larger society. In this chapter, however, I examine the wedding industry's growth, focusing on the history of White Crane Palace as an example of a more widespread process. I begin with a brief account of the diverse prewar wedding customs that the wedding industry's services have now almost universally replaced.

Prewar Diversity

Although I define the prewar period as roughly covering the first half of the current century, it is necessary to begin with practices that developed much earlier among the samurai, whose long period of dominance as Japan's ruling class greatly influenced subsequent trends in both weddings and marriage. It was the samurai, for example, who devised the *san-san-ku-do*, the *sake* exchange between bride and groom that forms the heart of the wedding ceremony. To be sure, the use of *sake* to seal a marriage is much older. The wedding ceremonial of the Heian period (794–1185) featured an exchange of *sake* between brides and grooms of the court nobility, long before the samurai seized political power. But the specific "three, three, nine times" pattern of the modern exchange derives from formal codes of etiquette that had developed among the samurai by the Muromachi period (1333–1573). Originally these codes were regimens of military training, developed by families recognized for their expertise in martial arts—the Ogasawaras, the most famous of these, were master horsemen and archers. Later the codes were expanded to cover all areas of dress and conduct.[1]

The wedding practices that thus came to be formalized show how the samurai differed from the Heian nobility in their norms of residence. At the Heian court, marriage did not always bring a change of residence for a woman, or the change might not come until years after the marriage was consummated. Wedding ceremonies were therefore held at the bride's house, although a reception at the groom's followed several days later. The samurai, however, stressed that marriage involved the bride's immediate transfer from her natal home to her husband's and they accordingly began the wedding preparations by selecting an auspicious day for the procession that would take the bride and her furnishings to her new home. The finality of her departure was marked by the building of a bonfire at the gate once she left—the same practice followed in funerals, after the corpse is removed from the house, to prevent the return of the departed family member. The wedding ceremony, consisting principally of the *san-san-ku-do*, was held on her arrival at the groom's home, where the reception that followed also took place.

New wedding practices arose among the samurai during the

political instability of the sixteenth century, when the country was divided among powerful warlords ruling autonomous domains. In these circumstances, arranging marriages became an important means of forging military alliances. This emphasis continued during the two and a half centuries of peaceful rule of the ensuing Tokugawa period (1603–1868). In this period the use of the nakōdo as a go-between became widespread, not only among the samurai, but also among urban commoners, who increasingly emulated samurai customs. The nakōdo also began to develop a reputation for exaggerating both parties' virtues and ignoring their faults, still cited in connection with those who fill the matchmaker's role.[2] The miai (literally, "see-meeting") became popular at this time as well, as a means of having the two parties meet before a decision was taken to enter formal negotiations. Prearranged by the nakōdo, and sometimes without the principals' foreknowledge, the miai typically took the form of a "chance" encounter during a family outing to admire the cherry blossoms or to dine at a restaurant, attend the theater, or patronize some other public place. Should both parties agree to the match, the couple was betrothed with a formal exchange of gifts called the *yuinō*. The food, *sake*, and clothing used as betrothal gifts, and the ceremony in which they were exchanged, became increasingly elaborate during the Tokugawa period. The ceremony that marks the engagement in most contemporary marriages still derives its name, plus many details of the exchange, from samurai custom.

As Japanese folklorists have long emphasized, different practices were common among the peasantry. According to evidence they began gathering in the early decades of this century, in many rural areas marriages were formerly not arranged by the parents but grew out of casual liaisons between young men and women, usually of the same village. There was also considerable variation in the timing of the bride's change of residence after marriage.[3] Sometimes she remained for a while in her natal home, receiving her husband's visits only at night, before finally going to live at his home—usually after the birth of a child or on his parents' retirement from active life. Sometimes her move was accomplished by degrees, beginning perhaps with a limited stay or with a series of daily visits in which she assisted in household chores. Wedding ceremonies also varied, sometimes taking place at the bride's home, sometimes at the groom's (or even at both), but generally involving a simple exchange of *sake*.

The Meiji period (1868–1912) brought many changes to the countryside, including the trend already seen in the cities of adopting customs that had originated among the samurai. These included the parental arrangement of marriage and the use of go-betweens to conduct negotiations, often over long distances. Reasons for these changes are diverse. The greater physical mobility of the population is said to have helped erode the isolation of rural villages and promote marriages over longer distances than before (Kamishima 1969: 82; Yanagita 1957: 167). Governmental policies also played a part, especially the promotion of traditional Confucian values through the newly instituted educational system, as a means of buttressing a sense of duty to the state. Many of these values encouraged parental control over the choice of marriage partners: the ethic of separation of the sexes, especially before marriage; the demand for chastity in women; and the strong support of parental authority (Dore 1958: 158–59). An additional factor in the spread of samurai customs was the lingering influence of the feudal hierarchy. In terms of the wedding ceremony itself, "The tendency to regard [practices] previously followed by the upper class as the real ceremony grew stronger, and unions not resulting from it came to seem less worthy somehow" (Yanagita 1967: 190). This process of emulating samurai custom extended to various details of ritual as prescribed by the Ogasawara or other schools of samurai etiquette. Embree's (1939: 203–10) description of the ideal he found current in Suye Mura, for example, includes the use of ceremonial nakōdo to formalize the betrothal, a wedding focusing on the bride's transfer to the groom's household, and a ceremony featuring the *san-san-ku-do* before the reception.

But not all weddings in Suye conformed to this ideal, proof that the spread of samurai-derived custom was still incomplete in rural Kyushu in the mid-1930s. Embree notes that most families skipped the formal betrothal, although this was explained as a consequence of its expense. But many families also dispensed with the big wedding celebration entirely, especially when the marriage was of a form clearly related to the older patterns described by the folklorists. Known locally as *mikka kasei* ("three days' labor"), this form of marriage involved a ceremony that was both smaller and less elaborate than usual—lacking the *san-san-ku-do* and using *shōchū*, a cheap distilled liquor, instead of *sake* (Smith and Wiswell 1982: 164–68). It also involved the bride's entering the groom's home for a brief stay, traditionally just three days, after which she returned temporarily to her natal home. The marriage might be broken off at this point if the experience was unsatisfactory, but in practice the bride almost always made the permanent move to her husband's home at a later date.[4]

If wedding customs in rural settings like Suye thus lacked uniformity during the prewar period, an even greater variation was developing in the cities. Home weddings based on formal Ogasawara-style etiquette—the pattern described by Embree as the rural ideal—were still quite common. One informant gave me an account of her own wedding in 1935 that matches this pattern perfectly. It was held in the home of her husband's family in Hirayama; upon her arrival in the evening,[5] the bride and the groom were wed in a ceremony featuring the *san-san-ku-do* and officiated by the nakōdo. The reception followed immediately and consisted of feasting and merrymaking that lasted most of the night. Neighbors of the groom's family assisted in preparing the food, although a professional caterer provided the fanciest dishes. As in rural areas, the celebrations lasted for three days, with various groups of people—friends, relatives, and neighbors—gathering at the house in succession.

But deviations from this pattern were also increasing by now. Perhaps because of the smaller size of urban houses, the custom of having the reception in a restaurant became fashionable for those who could afford it (Ema 1971: 215). A similar innovation was a religious ceremony held at a Shinto shrine, a practice that became popular after the first such ceremony was performed in 1900 for the wedding of the Crown Prince. This change enabled various combinations of locales for the wedding day's activities. A shrine ceremony could be followed by a reception at home, or a home ceremony might precede a reception at a restaurant. Or the entire proceedings could be held outside the home by having a shrine ceremony and a restaurant reception—the pattern Mrs. Shibata's account shows was still current in the early postwar period. Other informants who married at the same time chose a Shinto ceremony with a catered reception held on the premises of the shrine itself.

Once the activities of the wedding were divorced from their traditional place in the home, it became possible for commercial specialists to take ever-increasing control of the wedding's form. Ultimately this process produced the current pattern of wedding services, which quickly became predominant in urban areas before spreading out to encompass most of rural Japan as well. The result is a remarkable uniformity in contemporary weddings that contrasts sharply with the diversity of customs of the prewar period.

The Rise of the Wedding Industry

Commercially provided services are far from unique to the postwar wedding, to be sure. The Shinto ceremony may be regarded as such, for example, since from its inception shrines have charged a fee for its performance. And we have noted the services obtained from more specifically commercial establishments, such as restaurants and catering firms. Even in rural areas beauticians were involved in preparing the women's hair, especially that of the bride, and by the 1930s buses were commonly hired to transport the bride's party to the groom's home. Beauticians also frequently provided rented bridal costumes, although in the cities these were available from businesses specializing in clothing rentals (*kashi ishōya*) as well.

But none of these entrepreneurs provided anything approaching the range of services offered by the modern wedding industry. With the possible exception of clothing-rental shops, moreover, none depended on weddings for most of their business. The first specialists to become heavily committed to providing commercial services for weddings, as well as the first to provide a comprehensive set of services, were organizations known as *gojokai* ("mutual-aid clubs"). The growth of the wedding industry over the postwar period is intimately involved with the history of these organizations. The first gojokai was founded in Yokosuka in 1948 as a plan for guaranteeing low-cost weddings and funerals. Its inception and success resulted from concern about the costs of these ceremonies in the economically difficult years of the immediate postwar period. Under the initial plan of the Yokosuka gojokai, members paid installments of ¥15 a month, less than 0.2 percent of the average urban family's monthly income, over a period of ten years. In return members had the right to receive, on the occasion of either a funeral or a wedding, services provided by the gojokai and the use of certain ceremonial items it owned.[6]

The originator of this system had previously operated an undertaking business, and the plan was modeled after the modern style of funerary services that had developed in urban areas by that time. Funerary rites today begin as they always have with mourning services conducted in the home, transformed for that purpose by installing a special altar and other decorations. Formerly these items were owned communally by the neighbor- ✓ hood or village organization (Smith 1978: 216–17), but in urban areas it has long been common to rent them from the undertaker. The undertaker also makes arrangements for the disposal of the corpse and for catering the ensuing mortuary feast. Under the original gojokai plan, members received the undertaker's services and the loan of the funerary decorations at no extra charge. Weddings were incorporated under this plan by a similar arrangement. The gojokai owned a set of bridal robes that members were entitled to use for free. The gojokai also made arrangements on its members' behalf for all other services involved in holding the ceremony and reception.[7]

The first gojokai system thus did two things. By organizing the commercial aspects of weddings along lines already followed ① for funerals, it made a single organization responsible for providing a wide range of wedding-related services. The results of this innovation have been long lasting; the wedding industry still embodies this structure today. The second change has met a different fate, but one that is equally telling. The original gojokai system implemented an ideology emphasizing service for the ② common good of its members. The installment plan it introduced guaranteed them a predetermined, low price for its services, no matter how far into the future these might be deferred. This was one of its most attractive aspects in the early postwar years, a time of strong public concern over the waste of ceremonial expenditure.

The system continued to be appealing as a hedge against

rising wedding and funerary costs during the 1950s and early
1960s, a period that witnessed a gradual increase in the number
of companies modeled after the original. To a degree the initial
emphasis on serving the common good is still discernible in the
ideologies of gojokai companies today. The 1960s, however, saw
a significant change in the goals of gojokai organizations and in
their relationship to their members.[8] A key factor in this change,
and an important element in the tremendous growth of these organizations during the decade, was their decision to maintain
their own wedding halls. Wedding halls as such have a different
origin from gojokai companies; in the largest cities they date
back to the mid-1950s. But during the 1960s most gojokai became
actively involved in building their own halls, and the ready
availability of capital for such construction—in the form of members' dues—enabled them to become prominent as builders of
wedding facilities.

The changes in gojokai companies that began with the construction of their own facilities are illustrated by the history of
the origin of the Hirayama Gojokai, the parent company that
owns and operates White Crane Palace. This company, the first
gojokai in Hirayama, was founded in the early 1960s by Ishida
Tsuyoshi. Ishida, the owner of a small business making paper
umbrellas, noted the gradual decline in this industry in the postwar period and began to contemplate a new line of business. He
chanced to learn about the gojokai system on a visit to a neigh-
boring city and decided to start a similar company in Hirayama.
Soon he converted his umbrella workshop and warehouse into
an office for his new company, which he named the Hirayama
Gojokai. (In the following discussion, "the Gojokai" with a capital G always refers to this company.) The initial task of building
up membership involved long hours of door-to-door canvassing
of neighborhoods. But Ishida was strongly convinced of the
benefits of the gojokai system for its members, and in his sales
talks he stressed the dedication of the company to the common
good. He constantly repeated his motto, "All for one and one for
all," and asserted the company's goal of providing "solemn and
dignified ceremonies, without pretension or waste, for a small
monthly payment."

At first the Hirayama Gojokai simply made arrangements on
behalf of its members for services provided by other establish-

big growth

ments. After a year it had accumulated enough capital to purchase wedding costumes and various other items and to convert some of its facilities into a showroom where they could be displayed. All other services were still obtained elsewhere, but true to his belief in the goal of serving the common good, Ishida was very aggressive in securing for members the best services for the price. As the Gojokai grew and its revenues increased, the members' dues were used for building the Hirayama Wedding Palace, which was erected in 1965 on the site of Ishida's old workshop. It contained a room with a Shinto shrine for the ceremony, performed by a priest called in for the occasion, three tatami rooms, and a Western-style ballroom for receptions. Outside caterers provided the food, which Ishida continued to secure at the lowest possible prices for Gojokai members.

Hirayama Wedding Palace was unique in the city at the time of its opening. Longtime employees of the Gojokai assert that for many members it made receptions outside the home possible for the first time, since banquets at even modest restaurants were still beyond the means of many. For this reason, Ishida had little difficulty enrolling new members; people even came of their own to the company's office seeking permission to join. Soon the number of weddings began to strain the facilities. In 1968 a new wing with three more reception rooms was added, and the building was renamed White Crane Palace.

Membership in the Gojokai continued to increase by leaps and bounds; by the late 1970s over one-third of all the households in Hirayama were enrolled, and the wedding facilities had again been outgrown. In 1975 a larger and entirely new wedding hall was built, with the old facilities now used for more office space for the Gojokai. The new hall included a kitchen, eliminating the need to rely on outside catering services. By 1977 a new wing had to be added to handle the increasing volume of business. At the time of my fieldwork, the hall was performing over seven hundred weddings a year, roughly 30 percent of all those held in Hirayama.[9]

The expansion of the Gojokai's facilities has been accompanied by an increase in the number and range of wedding-related services it provides directly. This amalgamation of services has in turn contributed to a further expansion of facilities, a cycle of reinvestment whose starting point lies in the structure of the gojokai system itself. Because members prepay for services to be performed in the indefinite future, the Gojokai can apply its temporary surplus of capital to the construction of wedding facilities. Once built, these facilities themselves become a source of surplus capital.

The same cycle has also produced a gradual shift in the Gojokai's overall goals. The initial decision to construct a wedding hall was in keeping with the company's emphasis on serving its members' interests; its opening, as noted, enabled some members to have ceremonies they could not otherwise afford. But possession of its own facilities began to convert the Gojokai by degrees from the role of broker to that of entrepreneur. The addition of a kitchen at the new wedding hall in 1975 is a good example. It allowed the Gojokai to offer services directly, but also forced a commitment to the profitable use of that facility. The kitchen represents a loss if the staff remains idle, so White Crane Palace now caters all sorts of banquets to maintain a full work schedule. This has involved it in providing services to people other than Gojokai members, as indeed it had already begun to do with weddings by the time the new hall opened in 1975. Members are still entitled to special discounts,[10] but the services they receive are now available to all. The change in the Gojokai's role from broker to entrepreneur has had the effect of blurring the distinction between members and nonmembers; both have become customers.

This shift in the Gojokai's perspective, from an emphasis on service for its members' common good to one of profit making, has received further impetus from the increase in competition within the wedding industry. The demand for more sumptuous weddings has made the industry a highly lucrative and attractive business. White Crane Palace's initial success brought imitators, and by the time its new wedding hall opened, it was no longer the only such facility in the city. Not only had other wedding halls been established, but a number of hotels had begun to offer a similar range of services. Many of these establishments were in a good position to compete with White Crane Palace; some were more centrally located, and several—especially certain hotels—already enjoyed reputations for high-class service.[11] By 1980 White Crane Palace's growth had clearly begun to stall.

This slowdown has led the company to add still more services as a means of maintaining its competitive edge. It has added inexpensive honeymoon packages, for example, arranged through a travel agency, in the hope of convincing potential customers that White Crane Palace can offer them better services for less. But the competition has had a much broader impact: as the Gojokai has increasingly had to bend to market forces, it has also increasingly come to evaluate its activities from the economic perspective. Where the original gojokai ideology, formulated in a time of economic stress and uncertainty, made its goal the guarantee of low-cost ceremonies to those who could not otherwise obtain them, the current focus takes as its standard what is available elsewhere, not what people can or cannot afford.[12]

The Commercialized Wedding: Cost and Currency

The transformation of the Gojokai's goals points, above all, to the general acceptance of the commercialized wedding—the pattern of services described in Chapter 1. The characteristic elements of this pattern show a remarkable consistency in their occurrence at White Crane Palace, as illustrated in Table 1. Virtually all of the customers in the 228 weddings I checked received the services covered by the basic reception fee: the rental of the room; the provision of food and drink for the banquet, floral decorations for the tables, and bouquets used in the flower presentation; the printing of the invitations and seating charts. Note that the following services are not included in this fee, but were elected nonetheless in over 90 percent of the cases and are thus also part of the pattern: the Shinto ceremony, ironaoshi (indicating rental of the bridal costume), cake-cutting ceremony, candle service, photographs, hikidemono. Certain other commercial services that are probably equally prevalent, such as the bride's use of a beautician before the wedding, and the provision of wedding rings exchanged in the ceremony, should be included in the pattern. So should certain noncommercial aspects that are, in my experience, nearly universal: the use of the ceremonial nakōdo, of an emcee (who as the table shows is likely to be an amateur), of set kinds of speeches and songs.

How much does such a wedding cost? Table 1 lists prices for some of these elements, based on the brochure White Crane Pal-

TABLE 1

Frequencies and Costs of Wedding-Related Services,
White Crane Palace, 1982–83

(228 weddings)

Service	Frequency (percent)	Cost[a] (000 yen)
Ironaoshi[b]	99.6%	150+
Basic reception fee[c]	99.4	763
Photographs	99.4	10+
Hikidemono	99.4	3+
Flower presentation[d]	98.7	—
Candle service	96.1	15
Cake-cutting ceremony	95.6	10
Shinto ceremony[e]	93.9	30
Karaoke rental	43.9	3
Piano/organ rental	21.5	5+
Professional emcee	18.9	20

NOTE: The rate of exchange in this period was about $1 = ¥240.

[a]Costs are taken from White Crane Palace's brochure.

[b]Data for brides only. The cost is the minimum expenditure for renting 2 changes, chosen by 84.2% of the brides. Only 1 change of clothes was involved in 15.4% of the cases.

[c]Includes charges for food and drink, room rental, floral centerpieces, and miscellaneous expenses. Cost is calculated for the average level of services for a reception of 64 adults, the average size for the sample.

[d]The price of the bouquets is included in the basic reception fee. A few couples elected not to have this ceremony.

[e]The balance of the weddings involved nonreligious ceremonies held at White Crane Palace (0.9%) and services held elsewhere (0.4% Shinto, 1.3% Christian, 2.2% Buddhist).

ace gives potential customers. This information is not an accurate gauge of customers' expenditures, however: not only are most of the prices shown the minimum charges, but the list of services is incomplete. I did not collect data on actual wedding costs in deference to the staff's sensitivity about revenues. Fortunately, comparable data are available from the Sanwa Bank of Tokyo, which annually surveys newly wedded couples on how much they spent in getting married. Table 2 summarizes the data collected in 1982 on 410 couples, mostly living in the Tokyo and Osaka metropolitan regions. The total average expenditure of ¥6,853,000 ($28,554) includes the costs of the honeymoon and preparations for postmarital life, but even at ¥2,014,000 ($8,392), the wedding costs are still considerable. One can appreciate why the preferred wedding gift is cash: on average these couples received ¥1,509,000 ($6,288) in *shūgi* (congratu-

TABLE 2

Average Expenditures Relating to Marriage, June 1981–June 1982

(000 yen; 410 marriages)

Item	Cost
Betrothal	
Cash gifts	646
Other gifts	445
Miscellaneous	191
SUBTOTAL	1,282
Wedding	
Ceremony and reception	1,704
Gift to *nakōdo*	104
Miscellaneous	206
SUBTOTAL	2,014
Honeymoon	849
Preparations for married life	
Furniture, appliances, etc.	1,592
Change of residence	439
Clothing	677
SUBTOTAL	2,708
TOTAL	6,853

SOURCE: Sanwa ginkō [Sanwa Bank]. *Kekkon zengo no suitōbo* (Tokyo, 1982).

latory gifts), enough to defray three-fourths of the typical cost for the ceremony and reception.

Since the main focus of the Sanwa survey is expenditures, it does not provide much information on the type of wedding services selected. But there is reason to believe that most of these couples followed the pattern of services shown in Table 1. Informants who married at other commercial establishments, both hotels and wedding halls, and the testimony of wedding industry personnel I talked with in other cities support the conclusion that the commercialized wedding throughout Japan comprises essentially the same elements. On some measures, moreover, there is a close correlation between the Sanwa and White Crane Palace data: both show similar figures for the incidence of Shinto ceremonies (90.0 percent for Sanwa vs. 93.9 percent at White Crane Palace), for the proportion of brides having one or more ironaoshi (99.0 percent vs. 99.6 percent), and for the average number of guests at the reception (66.7 vs. 64.1).

These similarities are not so surprising when we consider the places chosen for weddings in the Sanwa sample (Table 3): wedding halls and hotels—the two main types of commercial competitors—account for approximately 70 percent of the weddings and receptions. Moreover, the pattern of services that characterize the commercialized wedding is not limited to strictly commercial institutions. The third-most-popular place for weddings, public meeting halls, includes facilities maintained by municipal governments and semipublic agencies like the Agricultural Cooperative. A decade ago these were even more frequently used for no-frill weddings in which the entire cost would be borne by the guests, a practice then seen especially by the young as offering a meaningful alternative to the standardized and elaborate commercial wedding.[13] Often these no-frills weddings served as a way for the couple to avoid financial reliance on their parents, and thus had a strongly individualistic and liberated flavor. The incidence of such simple weddings has declined, however; nowadays weddings performed at public meeting halls are more often direct imitations of those offered by the commercial industry—similar in content but slightly lower in price.[14]

Like public meeting halls, Shinto shrines have seen fit to accommodate themselves to the pattern of services developed in the commercial sector. Hirayama's largest and oldest shrine was the first to perform the Shinto wedding ceremony in the city, beginning in the early 1920's, and was one of only three shrines doing so at the time the Hirayama Gojokai opened its first facility in 1965. Its popularity declined with the growth of the commercial industry, though some couples continued to favor holding ceremonies there—followed by receptions in commercial facilities—because of its central place in the city's traditions, or because a parent or other relation had been married there. But by 1982 the ever-shrinking number of ceremonies prompted the shrine to construct a modern wedding facility on its own grounds, where it now offers receptions modeled on the commercial industry's pattern.[15]

If many of the weddings held outside the strictly commercial sector now resemble those found within, we may conclude that almost all of the Sanwa data reflect the same pattern of services. Indeed, weddings that appear to differ significantly are extremely

TABLE 3

Place of Wedding Ceremony and Reception

(Percent; 410 marriages)

Place	Ceremony	Reception
Wedding hall	40.5%	41.8%
Hotel	28.0	30.5
Public meeting hall	14.9	15.5
Shrine/temple	8.3	5.3
Church (domestic)	3.2	0.7
Church (overseas)	0.7	—
Home	0.2	0.5
Other	3.9	—
Not held	0.2	0.5

SOURCE: Same as Table 2.
   NOTE: Columns do not total 100 because of rounding and in the case of column 2, because there was more than 1 reception in 6 instances (1.5% of the sample).

few. Home weddings, probably the most common type of celebration before the war, are almost totally lacking in the sample (see Table 3). Christian weddings are also relatively few in number—note especially the low percentage of couples who chose to hold their reception in the church as well. And while one frequently hears of couples having church weddings performed in Hawaii to avoid the cost and trouble of a typical Japanese wedding, these too are numerically insignificant in the Sanwa data, which show that only 0.7 percent of all ceremonies were held in churches overseas.[16]

   A conservative estimate of the prevalence of the commercialized pattern in the Sanwa data would accordingly put it at 85 percent or more of the total. Although these data were obtained primarily from the two largest urban centers, I believe they indicate the general currency of the commercialized wedding in Japan. In Hirayama, for example, by rough estimate, wedding halls and hotels alone account for over 80 percent of all weddings. The wedding industry's aggressiveness, moreover, has ensured that the surrounding rural areas have been drawn into the urban commercial pattern: White Crane Palace maintains a small fleet of buses with which it brings in entire wedding parties from villages as much as 50 kilometers away in the surrounding mountain regions.[17] Smith (1978: 212–14) has described how by the mid-1970s such services had begun to erode the traditional pattern of home weddings in a rural hamlet in Shikoku.[18] In other parts of Japan such traditional weddings were still found in very remote regions in the early 1980s, but the acceptance of the commercialized wedding is so complete on the whole that I heard of none for the area around Hirayama.

THREE

The Actors

We have seen how the wedding industry's expansion has produced a uniform pattern of services, a commercially standardized script. Before turning to the symbolic content of that script, we must first learn more about the actors and the stage managers, and the influence they exercise on the script's performance. I begin this task in this chapter with a look at the events leading up to the wedding. For while these also follow a basic pattern, there is variation as well—much of it resulting from the conflicting perspectives of the principals and their parents. Formerly this conflict was held to correspond to the distinction between love matches (ren'ai) and marriages resulting from arranged introductions (miai), a dichotomy whose changing meaning over the postwar period therefore commands our attention.

The Changing Meaning of the Ren'ai/Miai Dichotomy

It will be recalled that the custom of having miai arose in conjunction with the emphasis on arranged marriage among the samurai, and that its later diffusion among the population was accompanied by a general increase in parental control over marriage. The English tag "arranged marriage" frequently applied to the term stems from these historical associations, although the practice itself has always consisted of arranging a preliminary meeting, not the engagement itself.

Parental control over marriage has greatly diminished since the war, and though such meetings are still frequent, the translation of miai as arranged marriage is nowadays totally inadequate. But in prewar years most marriages were indeed arranged in the literal sense of the word.[1] Partners were selected by the parents in consultation with relatives or friends of their own generation, who were instrumental in conducting negotiations with the other family. In theory a child had the right to veto a particular choice based on the brief impressions formed at the miai, but in practice family pressure often overrode individual protest.

One reason for this strong parental role was frequently the young people's own lack of confidence in matters regarding the opposite sex. Relations between the sexes were much more restricted, in keeping with the Confucian precept that "a boy and girl must not sit together after they are seven years of age." Many of my older informants confirmed that before the war unmarried men and women could not walk together without fear of damaging their reputations. Even those who married in the early 1950s often had so little experience with the other sex that they relied on the opinions of elders, rather than trust their own judgment in selecting a spouse.

Another reason for the strength of parental influence was the importance of marriage to the interests of the family. For one thing, marriage indexed the family's social standing, since matches tended to follow lines of class and occupational status closely (Embree 1939: 161). For another, it directly affected the family's well-being when it involved a spouse for the heir of the household (ie). In those cases the incoming member was expected to become both a contributor to the family enterprise and the source of its future generations. The health, character, personal abilities, and family background of a prospective partner were therefore thoroughly investigated by a person's parents, and the decision to marry based primarily on their findings. Such matters were considered far more important than the child's personal preferences.

But the larger significance of parental control over marriage lay precisely in its congruence with prewar values stressing the subordination of the individual to the larger group. Accepting the parents' choice in marriage ratified the basic values of society, and to do otherwise was a serious matter indeed. Thus Dore's finding, in his early 1950s study of Tokyo, that before the war couples who decided to marry on their own usually took measures to secure parental permission, is not surprising. Nor is his comment that "a 'good' girl might never allow her parents to know that it was all a put-up job when the go-between appointed by the groom's family came to ask for her hand." But while he notes that "the presence of such a go-between is an essential for the social recognition of the marriage," it was rather the miai that came to symbolize the socially proper union. Perhaps this was because it more clearly indicated that the parents' perspective was being favored: "'Arranged marriage' (*miai kekkon*) means that the parties were brought together expressly for the purpose of marriage on the initiative of parents, a friend of the family or a go-between. It means also that the initial criteria of selection were objective ones" (Dore 1958: 165–67).

If, by contrast, love marriages were "generally disapproved," as Smith (1956: 77) observed for rural Shikoku, it is not because prewar society was uncognizant of romantic love. Indeed, love is one of the "human feelings" that the prewar Japanese celebrated and cultivated—while insisting that it remain in its proper place (Benedict 1946: 183–85). For men, amorous female companionship was available from prostitutes and geisha, and such pursuits were not considered improper so long as they did not interfere with other responsibilities. Love similarly had a place in the adolescent years preceding marriage, one that Smith and Wiswell's look at prewar Suye Mura shows was much more extensive than commonly thought. But even in this intimate village realm, replete with gossip of the love letters and romances of the young, considerations of love and marriage were clearly separate:

Writing letters, talking to young men, being in love with someone— all that is fun. It is amusing when you are young, and so you do it, but when the time comes to marry you stop it, discard all the letters, and follow the wishes of your parents. That is quite a different matter. You do not expect to marry the man you correspond with, and love and marriage are not thought of as being related (Smith and Wiswell 1982: 119).

Sometimes attempts were made to formalize romantic relationships with the use of a go-between, as Dore found in his Tokyo study. In Suye pregnancy often forced the issue. But no amount of negotiation could succeed if the difference in social status between the lovers was too great. Marriage was rarely the outcome, for example, between a son of the household and the servant he got pregnant; the girl was expected to accept a hastily arranged marriage with someone more suitable (Smith and Wiswell 1982: 130–36).

Those who refused such matches and insisted on marrying for love alone risked total loss of social support: "True love matches are rare. When they do occur, the couple usually goes out on their own" (Smith and Wiswell 1982: 154). The consequence of such action was understandably severe, since it meant putting individual interest above that of the collectivity, thereby defying the basic principles of prewar morality. Dore (1958: 161) notes that one intellectual who defied those principles in the 1920s by arguing for "marriage as the culmination of love, and love as a condition of marriage," was attacked, appropriately, with "moral fury." Like its opposite term miai, then, ren'ai was invested with ideological significance, and in the strongly hierarchical values of prewar Japan its connotations were decidedly negative.

The revised Civil Code of the postwar era removed most of the legal support for the ie and its head, and parental authority was dealt a further blow by Article 24 of the Constitution, which declared that marriage was to be "based only on the mutual consent of both sexes." Since these legal changes were expected eventually "to weaken the concept of marriage as a duty toward the house" in popular thought, the dichotomy between ren'ai and miai took on a new meaning—that of social barometer. By 1950 the increase in the proportion of ren'ai marriages after the war was already being interpreted as an indication of the spread of individualistic values (Steiner 1950: 299). Similar conclusions were drawn from surveys showing a preference among the young for relying on their own rather than parental opinion in selecting a spouse (Baber 1958; Yamamuro 1960).

But even as such studies were being made, the assumed contrast between the two forms of marriage was becoming less meaningful. In the early 1950s marriages begun through miai introductions were giving increasing importance to individual preference. Dore (1958: 165–68) reports that young people were commonly sent off by themselves after the meeting, and they might even enjoy a period of private courtship lasting weeks or months as a basis for reaching a decision to marry. True love matches, meanwhile, were becoming less individualistic than in the past. Although the percentage of marriages openly labeled

as such was increasing, they were just as likely to include negotiations using relatives or go-betweens to formalize the relationship as their prewar predecessors—those marriages that had
begun on an individual basis, but were made to look as though
they had been arranged according to family interests.

Both forms of marriage had thus come to include significant
interaction at two levels: as a personal relationship between the
principals and through formal negotiations conducted by their
families. By the late 1950s this parallelism was making the distinction between ren'ai and miai difficult to apply. When, in
1958–59, Blood asked some 400 couples in Tokyo to classify their
marriages, he found one-fourth of them could not do so without
qualifications that stressed the mixed nature of their experience.
Unions that began through a miai introduction but later blos-
somed into passionate love did not seem to the couples to be accurately described as miai marriages; couples whose families
had conducted formal negotiations for a relationship that began
casually were equally reluctant to think of their cases as typical
ren'ai affairs (Blood 1967: 13–34).[2]

Interviews I conducted with newly married couples suggest
that for many this mixture of the individual and the familial perspective in both forms of marriage has completely robbed the
distinction of its former ideological significance. One man in his
early twenties was puzzled when he was asked if he preferred
marriage by ren'ai or miai. To him the two represented not
moral alternatives, but merely successive strategies. As he saw
it, most people have one or more casual relationships when
young, and perhaps one of these develops into marriage of the
ren'ai type. If not, they begin having formal introductions—
miai meetings—to ensure they will find a partner before their
age makes marriage extremely difficult.

If this young man's pragmatic attitude shows that the difference between the two forms of marriage no longer carries ideological weight, his response reveals a moral stance nonetheless,
of which he is perhaps unaware. It is a stance, moreover, that
points out the continuing contrast between Japanese and Western values regarding the individual. Complete autonomy im-
plies that the individual is free to remain single should he or she
choose to do so, yet the Japanese insist that marriage is necessary for social recognition as fully adult. I look at the implica-

tions of this view in a later chapter. Here I only point out that the Japanese marry with much greater regularity than the citizens of other developed nations do. This helps explain the continuing value for the Japanese of the miai, the subject to which we now turn.

Miai Marriages: Contemporary Forms

Miai meetings normally occur after both parties have given their preliminary consent based on evaluations of each other's background. Although considerations of a family's history and social standing were formerly important enough to warrant the use of professional investigators at times (Dore 1958: 168; Ema 1971: 171), nowadays objective evaluation is usually limited to information learned through the mediator.[3]

Mediation comes about in two ways. The family of a son or daughter may ask a third party, usually someone likely to have a wide range of social contacts, to begin looking for a suitable partner; or a mediator may suggest a possible match to the family on his or her own initiative. In either instance the mediator is usually someone close enough to the family to be familiar with its situation. The cases of two of my informants illustrate the process leading to the initial meeting.

Case 1. Satō Fumio, age thirty, works as a salesman for a large company that manufactures electronics equipment. He is the youngest of three children; his older brother and sister are both already married. His brother has been running a store in another city for over fifteen years, but intends to return eventually to live with his parents and care for them in their old age. This freed Fumio, who lived at home until he got married, from having to ask potential partners to share these responsibilities, which would have hampered his marital chances.

Fumio started having miai encounters about three years before his marriage, when his parents made a few informal requests to friends to start looking for a suitable partner. One of the people they asked is a woman who runs a rice store with her husband. Because she regularly goes to her customers' homes on deliveries, she has a good idea of the household situations of a number of families and accordingly is in a good position to serve as a clearing house for such information. Furthermore, she

appears to enjoy arranging matches, having successfully performed this role a number of times in the past. The miai meeting
that resulted in Fumio's marriage was one of several she arranged for him.

Fumio described the procedure that led to his miai meetings
in the following manner. The matchmaker brought the prospect's photograph and a brief personal history to his home,
having previously secured the same materials from Fumio to
distribute to families with daughters looking for husbands. The
photograph and personal history were examined by Fumio and
his parents, who then informed the matchmaker whether they
wished to proceed with an arranged meeting. Ideally this decision is based on such social considerations as the educational
level and occupations of the other person's family, including any
brothers and sisters. The purpose is ostensibly to ensure that
differences in background or social position would not pose
a serious barrier to close interaction between the two families.
In actuality the Satōs never turned down an offer on these
grounds; those cases that never made it to the first meeting were
always rejected because Fumio did not like the woman's appearance. Others were turned down after the first meeting for different reasons, including his parents' reservations about the
woman's personality, and once because of information from
an independent source about the young woman's undesirable
qualities—she was reported to be excessively fond of drinking.

Case 2. Ōta Yoshie, age twenty-nine, lived at home with her
mother until her marriage. Her father died when she was nine-
teen, and since then her mother has continued running the family's small clothing store. She has one brother, now in his first
year as a university student, who is expected to return after
graduation and shoulder the responsibility of caring for their
mother. Yoshie was therefore free to marry out. Since graduating from high school, she had worked mostly in the family
store, but had occasionally taken a temporary job outside.

Yoshie had seventeen miai before her introduction to her husband a little over a year ago. The earliest took place when she
was only twenty and not ready to consider marriage seriously;
and it did not come at her family's request. Her mother did begin
to make such requests a few years later, when Yoshie was twenty-
three, and from that time on she had miai meetings regularly

over a five-year period. She knew of several people—both men and women—who had over twenty miai meetings, and thus did not think her case extraordinary. The real reason for such large numbers, she believes, is the presence of someone close to the family who enjoys matchmaking and keeps up a steady supply of prospects. Since there was more than one matchmaker type in her case, miai opportunities often came in bunches, making it necessary to have a meeting with one candidate before making a firm refusal of the previous one. Strictly speaking this was improper; Yoshie admitted the would-be matchmakers and their candidates would have been displeased had they found out. Like Fumio, she rejected a number of prospects before the first meeting, some based on the photograph alone, others because she or her mother objected to the man's personal history. Sometimes they considered the man's job unsteady, and in one instance the man was shorter than she. Obviously, the matchmaker who brought the photograph and personal history could easily have recognized such a purely objective obstacle as the woman's being taller than the man, but Yoshie commented that those who enjoy this role do not always look that closely before recommending a match.

Meetings and Beyond: Ways to Refuse or Accept

Once the decision to have a meeting is made from these preliminary evaluations, the rest of the miai process is largely given over to the principals. They are left to explore their reactions to each other through a series of dates that begins with the initial encounter and continues until some decision has been reached. At the same time and at another level, the matchmaker is often playing a pivotal role in the delicate matter of accepting or rejecting the match. I continue with the accounts of the two cases introduced above to illustrate the process.

Case 1 (continued). Fumio asserts that the place and format of the initial meeting are usually determined by the matchmaker, who is likely to have his or her preferences about the degree of formality and the type of setting. The miai that led to his own marriage, however, followed his family's preference for a meeting at their home, something they had done several times previously. Fumio declares that it really did not matter to him where

these meetings were held, but says he does find it more difficult
to relax in a neutral place such as a restaurant or hotel. He also
believes that showing the other party one's home is more open
and honest, since it gives them the opportunity to observe one's
lifestyle directly.

The content of this particular meeting conformed to the general pattern. Unlike most Japanese gatherings, miai meetings
do not begin with a formal statement of purpose; instead, the
matchmaker simply introduces the two families. This formality
is followed immediately by small talk about neutral subjects
such as the weather, carried on mostly among the parents. The
two parties usually sit with parents directly opposite parents,
and the young man and woman facing each other. Because the
purpose of the meeting is explicitly to consider marriage, the
mood is tense. Despite a strong desire (on the man's part at
least) to look closely at the other person, the strain of the moment forces both to look modestly downward, catching at best a
few quick glimpses. Occasionally the conversation turns directly
to one of the young people, who tries to make as brief a comment as possible. After a while someone suggests that the two
go off somewhere in private. Once they leave, it is up to the man
to take the lead; he usually proposes that they go to a coffee
shop or somewhere they can talk. Fumio prefers to go for a drive.

If either party decides to refuse, this usually occurs by the
couple's third meeting. Extending the relationship past this point
is tricky. If the man has still not agreed, his family is obliged to ask
the matchmaker for more time to think things over, and with
this he runs the risk of appearing indecisive and being rejected
by the woman's family on that ground alone. Simply refusing
is a difficult matter in itself, and one of the matchmaker's most
important functions is to present a refusal in a way that injures
neither party. For men there is an additional problem: it is considered impolite to refuse, because women are thought to be
delicate and easily hurt by an outright rejection. In one case
Fumio came up with his own solution to this predicament: while
taking the young woman out for a drive he intentionally drove
as close to the side of the road as possible, so that she could not
help feeling uncomfortable each time they approached a tele-
phone pole or some other obstacle. Fumio figured this unpleas-

ant experience alone was enough to ensure his rejection by the woman. She in fact did turn down the marriage shortly afterward, although he of course does not know her real reason for doing so.

In the case of the miai leading up to his marriage, Fumio decided by the end of the third meeting to give an affirmative answer. He did not express this directly but relayed it through the matchmaker, which he and others say is the normal channel. The young woman did not share this view, however. She declared that it was insufficient to receive such information through a third party and insisted on hearing Fumio himself express his intention to marry her. Fumio complied, although he has since reflected that this was his first indication of how assertive a person his wife has turned out to be.

Case 2 (continued). Yoshie's introduction to her husband Toshinori did not come from any of the people her family had asked to look for prospective partners, who had been responsible for most of her previous seventeen miai meetings. The mediator this time was a friend of Toshinori's sister's husband. He had been asked to look for someone on Toshinori's behalf, and by chance is also an acquaintance of Yoshie's grandfather, who lives next door to Yoshie and her mother. After exchanging photographs, both sides agreed to an initial meeting, leaving it up to the mediator to arrange the details. The meeting took place in the early evening at Yoshie's grandfather's house. Toshinori was accompanied by the mediator alone. He did not go with his parents, he explains, because of his dislike of fuss and formality, and in fact all seven of his prior miai had resulted from informal introductions made by people fairly close to his own age. He considers his meeting with Yoshie to be typical of his experiences.

On entering the house for the miai, he was introduced to Yoshie's grandfather, who engaged him in small talk for a while because, according to Toshinori, he wanted to see what kind of a person Toshinori was. Yoshie came in shortly, and soon her grandfather instructed them to go off by themselves for a while. Since Toshinori prefers situations where he can relax, he took Yoshie to a restaurant run by one of his friends, where they had dinner and a few drinks. The two found they enjoyed each other's company, and it was not until 10:00 or so that he took her back home. This was rather late for the first meeting of a miai;

Toshinori said the proper thing is to agree on a second meeting and take the woman home early, but since they had been drinking, they had not paid much attention to the time.

The next time they met Toshinori decided he liked Yoshie enough to marry her. He did not tell her immediately, saying only on parting that he would express his feelings at their next meeting, and that she should be psychologically prepared. In fact she was not ready when he proposed directly at their third meeting, having assumed he would only suggest that they continue seeing each other. She asked at first for time to think it over, but by the end of the meeting had accepted. Toshinori says that he proposed directly because he objected to the normal arrangement of reaching agreement at the initiative of the person who made the introduction. Matchmakers usually ask both parties for their impressions after the second or third meeting. They will then often relay the responses in a suggestive manner, according to Toshinori, such as, "The other side seems favorably inclined, how about you?" After he and Yoshie reached their own agreement, however, he followed form by telling the mediator he was in favor of the match and asking him to so inform Yoshie's family.

Choosing the Miai Strategy: Who and Why

Although statistics on miai marriages show a gradual decline in the postwar period, they still account for about a third of the total.[4] The statistics cannot tell us, though, who gets involved in these marriages, or why. For this information I rely on the impressions of informants, who point to several factors as relevant to the adoption of a miai strategy.

As already suggested, age is important. Most young people prefer to find a partner by themselves, but as they grow older and it becomes clear that their chances of meeting suitable prospects on their own are poor, they usually slide into the miai pattern. The Japanese have strong views on the age at which a young person should marry. The word *tekireiki*, "appropriate age," specifically refers to the appropriate age for marriage—the range of years when one ought to get married, and past which it becomes increasingly difficult to find a partner. The range for women is twenty-two to twenty-five, and for men, twenty-six to thirty (Prime Minister's Statistical Office 1979: 577). Pressure to have miai meetings begins to increase as people approach the upper ends of these ranges. Toshinori, who was thirty-three at the time of his miai with Yoshie, says his family and relatives had been urging him to have such meetings for several years. Other male informants who also married late agree that once past thirty, the pressure to marry becomes increasingly difficult to ignore.

The reasons some people fail to marry by the time they approach the upper limit of the tekireiki vary. As in our society, some men and women are simply not well suited to finding partners on their own. They may be shy or unattractive; they may hold unrealistically high standards or have soured on romance because of a bad relationship in the past. And some, like Toshinori, who describes himself as "easygoing," are not in any particular hurry to marry. He regarded the whole business as something of a bother.

But some of the reasons for delayed marriages are more specific to Japan. Early in the postwar period the lack of "established patterns of courtship" limited the number of ren'ai marriages (Dore 1958: 170), and chances for the young to socialize with members of the opposite sex are still few in comparison with Western countries. Attending college, for example, offers less opportunity for social mixing than in the West. Although a third of Japanese women now go on to higher education, most attend all-female junior colleges. By contrast the four-year colleges that attract the men who continue on are predominantly a male domain. For most young people the workplace offers the greatest chance for interacting with the opposite sex, but the range of contacts may be limited and does not change appreciably after a person settles into a routine. Interest groups, such as clubs for devotees of various sports, arts, or other leisure activities, and private schools for lessons in foreign languages, calligraphy, or the martial arts, are another way of meeting people of the opposite sex. Apart from this, the list of possibilities is short indeed, especially since domestic arrangements place significant limits on contacts. Most women live at home until they marry. A higher percentage of men move out, usually for reasons related to their jobs, but most live either in all-male company dormitories or in tiny one-room apartments.

For some, stigmatization for one reason or another reduces the chances of marriage. Close interaction with members of certain religious sects is generally avoided by the rest of society, for example.[5] For the members of these religions themselves, moreover, there is considerable family pressure to marry within the sect, and miai arranged with other members are frequent. Other people are adversely affected by their domestic situation. Having only one parent can be considered a disadvantage; this is perhaps one reason for the anxiety that prompted Yoshie's mother to arrange miai for her well before she approached the end of the tekireiki.

The responsibility of caring for parents can also be a disadvantage. Formerly this obligation fell to the household head's successor, who remained in the house after marriage. Despite the abolition of the ie's legal status, many Japanese parents continue to value intergenerational continuity of the household unit and prefer to reside with one of their married children. For others it is a matter of economic necessity, since pensions and government social welfare programs often fail to provide people with adequate financial support in their old age. Whatever the reason, filial duty commits many Japanese to share households with their parents, though it is common nowadays for the younger married couple to spend some years living separately before eventually moving in. As in the prewar period, the preference continues to be for the eldest son (*chōnan*) to fill this role, although it is often assumed by one of the other family members instead.

The matter of who is ultimately to take care of the parents is not always settled at the time of a child's marriage, but when the decision is made it affects the marriage chances of all the siblings. Men who agree to fill the traditional role of the chōnan are at a disadvantage. Although some young women declare their lack of concern, many state flatly that their ideal marriage partner is someone without the chōnan's responsibilities. They would rather avoid the strain of living with their husband's parents, no matter how far into the future that may be deferred. Of course this does not prevent many from marrying a chōnan with whom they have fallen in love after a chance encounter. But others consistently refuse to enter into a serious relationship with anyone having this responsibility. Men who assume the chōnan role are

thus more likely to have difficulty in finding a partner by themselves and more apt to be forced to seek miai meetings as they
get older.

The question of the parents' care becomes all the more press-
ing when there are no sons in the family. In prewar Japan, when
that happened the ie's legal duty to secure a male heir required
the adoption of a son, who usually married a daughter of the
family and remained with her in the household. Grooms who
consent to the responsibility of caring for their wives' parents
are still frequently adopted in this manner, giving up their own
surnames in what continues to be popularly designated a *muko-
tori* ("husband-taking") marriage—as opposed to the normal
yome-iri ("bride-entering") marriage. But the husband's weak
position within the family structure has long made this type of
marriage notoriously unattractive. Fewer parents nowadays will
demand that a daughter shoulder such a responsibility, analo-
gous to the chōnan's, and be forced to seek a husband who
would consent to this undesirable arrangement. Women faced
with such demands are at a considerable disadvantage in finding
a partner and are therefore much more likely than most to resort
to miai.[6]

There are some single people for whom even the miai strategy
proves inadequate, and they are likely to broaden the search by
using a formal matchmaking service (*kekkon sōdanjo*).[7] In these
operations applicants submit their photographs; information on
their families and on their own education, employment history,
and personal interests and tastes; and a statement on the qualities they are looking for in a mate. The agencies then use this
information as a basis for recommending likely matches with
other clients. Matchmaking services are regarded as a last resort
and are used by those who have let the tekireiki slip by, or who
would obviously have trouble finding a suitable partner in the
first place. High proportions of the applicants are either chōnan
who wish a bride to move in with their family or daughters of
families desiring an in-marrying husband.

The Contemporary Ren'ai Process

Like marriages resulting from miai meetings, love matches involve interaction at two separate levels, one individual and the

other familial. The time sequence is reversed, however, since the couple's personal relationship precedes the negotiations to secure parental consent for the match. Love matches are therefore thought to give more consideration to the pair's feelings in the decision to marry, and therein lies their attraction for the young. One newly wedded woman summed up this appeal in one word—*tokimeki*, the throbbing of an impassioned heart.

Love matches are also considered more casual, since the initial encounter is usually neither mediated by a third party nor preceded by any sort of screening process. As the following cases illustrate, however, there is considerable variation in both the extent to which such relationships develop as casual affairs and the extent to which the decision to marry is based on passion rather than objective considerations.

Case 3. Hasegawa Hiroshi and Keiko, both twenty-five, first met almost six years ago through a chance encounter at the apartment of a mutual friend. Both were sophomores at the same university in Tokyo at the time; thus it was their student experience that brought them together, since their homes are in widely separated regions of Japan. They saw each other continually from then on, but it was not until they approached graduation in their senior year that they began to talk seriously about marriage.

Keiko claims she took most of the initiative in their decision, which she paradoxically attributes to a weakness rather than a strength of character. She had been willing to marry Hiroshi all along, she says, although marriage had never figured into their relationship from the beginning, and Hiroshi had not shown any sign of wanting to make it permanent. But she had not seen any point in trying to settle the issue while they were still students. The uncertainties involved were too great: she felt she could not be sure what Hiroshi's ultimate intentions would be, given his unpredictable and slightly cantankerous personality; she was also conscious of the tendency for student lovers to part at graduation, especially when faced with family pressure to return to homes that are far apart.

But as graduation neared and the prospect of parting became imminent, she felt a strong desire to remain with Hiroshi. When she expressed her feelings openly, Hiroshi resisted making a definite commitment, claiming that he could not even imagine what marriage would be like or the magnitude of the responsibilities involved. Moreover, he had decided to return home to Hirayama and try for a job as a civil servant; he knew there was no chance of getting into the civil service right away, since the exams were highly competitive, and it might be several years before he finally passed. In the meantime he would have to settle for temporary or part-time work, which would not give him enough security to marry. He wanted Keiko to return home and stay with her parents until he was sure of getting a secure job. She refused, complaining that it would greatly increase the distance between them. She insisted on remaining in Tokyo and arranged to move in with a friend who was also planning to stay on after graduation. This finally changed Hiroshi's mind, because he felt that Tokyo was not a good place to leave a woman alone. He agreed to inform his parents of their intention to marry and to ask people he knew in Hirayama to help them find a place to live and a job for Keiko.

Keiko characterizes her refusal to return home as "selfish." It was this act, however, based on her strong personal feelings, that finally triggered the pair's decision—after a relationship that truly grew out of a casual meeting and had continued for over two years before they seriously considered the question of marriage. By contrast, the next couple I introduce began their relationship with marriage already in mind and gave considerable weight to objective criteria in deciding to marry.

Case 4. Kobayashi Satoru, thirty-three, and Hiroko, thirty, both work for a large manufacturing firm in Hirayama. They had met at their company on several occasions over the years, but none of these encounters led to any subsequent relationship. In the summer before their marriage, however, Satoru asked Hiroko to participate in a camping trip he was organizing among company personnel. His decision to invite her even though he did not know her very well was based on his awareness of her interest in outdoor sports, and also on the fact that he was having difficulty finding enough participants to make the trip economically feasible.

During the two-day trip they decided to get married. The abruptness of the decision prompted Hiroko to characterize the marriage as similar to a miai affair, although both of the Kobayashis agree that, strictly speaking, it should be classed as ren'ai.

To Hiroko ren'ai means having a relationship with someone and then deciding to marry, whereas in their case they decided to get married without having a relationship first. It was therefore similar to a miai because she ended up marrying someone she did not know well at all. But both contend that the suddenness of the decision was understandable, given their situations. They had both passed the tekireiki and for several years had been under considerable pressure from their families to get married. Also, their company is one of the most prestigious in Hirayama and therefore one of the most highly competitive in its hiring. Firms like theirs check carefully on an applicant's background, so the successful applicant is certain to be of good family, well educated, and intelligent, and to come with good recommendations about his or her character. Accordingly, both felt that much of the selection process had already been completed for them, and they could hardly go wrong in choosing a co-worker as a spouse. Satoru had also wanted to marry someone who shares his interest in outdoor sports; Hiroko states that she simply wanted to get married in a hurry, before she turned thirty.

Hiroko is doubtless exaggerating the capriciousness of her decision. She and Satoru have a number of things in common other than their employer and their "advanced" age. Both share scientific backgrounds, for example: Hiroko is a graduate of a pharmaceutical college and works in the company's clinic, and Satoru is an engineer in the computer division. She was probably waiting for someone like Satoru, who respects her intelligence, training, and desire to pursue a career. Regardless of the degree to which these considerations figured in her decision, Hiroko's comparison of the match to a miai marriage is justified on two counts: both principals were prompted by their ages to think about marriage before the relationship began, as is usually true in the miai process, and both relied heavily on objective criteria in making their decision.

The final case I introduce illustrates that some ren'ai marriages may not be all that appropriate if judged by objective factors alone.

Case 5. Takagi Ichirō, twenty-eight, is from Komagatake, a small mountain resort outside Hirayama, where he lived with his parents until his marriage. His family runs a modest inn that features baths supplied by water from a nearby hot spring, the major attraction of the area. Ichirō has been working in the family business since he was graduated from high school. He enjoys the leisurely work schedule, which gives him ample free time during the day, although he is rarely able to take a day off, much less an extended holiday. It has always been understood in his family that Ichirō, the eldest son, would remain at home and take on the responsibility of looking after his parents.

Akiko, also twenty-eight, is from Hirayama. After graduating from college, she took a job as an elementary teacher in Fujisato, a small village in the mountains about ten kilometers downstream from Komagatake. She taught there for three years before transferring to a school in Hirayama itself. The couple first met at the Fujisato school's sports festival shortly after Akiko started teaching there, but the meeting was entirely casual and did not lead to any subsequent encounters. They met again more than two years later, about ten days before Akiko was due to leave for Hirayama. This meeting was also casual, the result of an introduction by a mutual friend, and it led to two dates before Akiko's departure.

Soon after Akiko moved to Hirayama, Ichirō came to see her and immediately proposed marriage. She was completely taken by surprise, since nothing in their relationship had indicated he was thinking of such a thing. She told Ichirō that his proposal was premature, and that in any case she was not disposed to get married at all. She had been in love once before, she explained, but the relationship ended without the man ever clearly responding to her affection. Accordingly, she felt it unlikely she would ever meet anyone she could love again and was determined she would never marry.[8] Ichirō replied that he would wait until she changed her mind.

From then on he began to see her frequently, at first telephoning her on days they would not meet, but later making the one-and-a-half-hour drive from Komagatake every day to see her in the evening, a pattern of courtship he maintained for an entire year. His persistence eventually paid off. Akiko finally gave her consent to a marriage that, as she herself notes, was highly inappropriate for purely objective reasons. Normally, if there is any difference in social status, the groom's is higher than the bride's, but in this case Akiko's position was clearly higher than Ichirō's. She had graduated from a university and he had not, and beyond that, as a teacher she is in a profession that is particularly well respected in the kind of rural district where his family lives. Ichirō's parents in fact tried to discourage him from pursuing the relationship for this reason, arguing she was too good for him and would never consent to be his bride. Ichirō simply told them that he would keep trying.

An additional reason for Akiko's initial reticence, and another factor that made the match seem so improbable in the first place, is that Ichirō clearly had the obligation of looking after his parents and continuing both the household and the family business. Akiko sees this as meaning that sooner or later she will have to give up her career as a teacher. At some point she must move in with his family, and she feels she will be unable to continue as a teacher in a household where everyone else is busy with the family enterprise.

Ichirō's remarkable persistence was spurred by an awareness of his limited prospects for finding a good marriage partner in his remote mountain district. He was convinced that he would never meet anyone as highly qualified as Akiko again, and the fact that she was by objective criteria probably too good to consider marrying him did not lessen his determination to win her with his romantic attentions.

The Matter of Approval

Once the principals have reached their own decision to marry, they face the task of securing their parents' approval. Ordinarily parents are aware of the seriousness of their son's or daughter's relationship and have met the prospective partner before the subject of marriage is formally brought up. Many have already given some indication of their disposition toward the match. The couple is thus in a good position to anticipate their parents' reaction, and in most cases consent can be taken for granted. But the matter of approval does not end here: an additional and important step is involved, one that is best understood historically, and in terms of its structural parallel with the miai process.

In prewar miai marriages most of the interaction took place at the interfamilial level, the principals often having but a single meeting before the decision to marry. This decision also lay primarily at the level of interfamilial negotiations. If the man's parents were satisfied with the outcome of their investigations and with the impressions they received at the miai, they sent the go-between (or perhaps an older male relative) as their representative to make a formal proposal to the woman's parents. Although the principals were asked during the proceedings if they objected to the match, they took no direct part in the negotiations. The increasing emphasis in the postwar period on the couple's personal feelings has resulted in the incorporation of individual interaction in the miai process, and a corresponding shift in the locus of the final decision. Along with these changes, the formal visit to petition the woman's parents has been abandoned.

As we have seen, in prewar times the use of such visits to formalize a relationship after the fact was critical for gaining social recognition of the match. This continued to be true after the war as well; male informants who married in the 1950s and 1960s say they followed the same procedure, sending a representative to ask the woman's parents for their consent. The incorporation of this visit as a regular feature of the ren'ai process no doubt played an important part in the increasing popularity of love matches. But it also meant that marriage was not becoming a strictly individual matter despite the growing number of ren'ai, for when it came time to formalize the match, the decision was still very much a family affair. As in the miai process of that time, the principals themselves had no part in the negotiations and in fact were not even supposed to be present.

The family of one informant who married by ren'ai in 1967 tells of the conflict between this practice and the changing conditions of modern life. His family asked an uncle and another man to represent it in seeking the approval of his sweetheart's parents. Private automobiles had become common enough for their use to be felt appropriate for such important transactions, but neither of the two older men could drive. The groom-to-be therefore had to serve as driver for the twenty-five-mile trip to the woman's home, but was sternly warned by his mother not to enter his intended's house under any circumstances because it was not his place to do so.

By this date, too, or a little later, the young people themselves began to have their own ideas about the proper way to seek the families' approval. An informant who married in 1972, for example, felt bold enough to go by himself to ask for his intended's hand—only to meet with a refusal from his future father-in-law to receive such a request unless it came from the proper representative, someone of his own generation. Approval was eventually granted, but not until the suitor returned with an older relative who did most of the talking. In a matter of years, even that formality was being dropped. Most young men now go by themselves to seek the parents' consent to the match. Rarely does such a request meet with disapproval. Formerly, in both ren'ai and miai marriages, consent was withheld at the initial request on the grounds that a certain amount of time was needed for proper consideration. But I heard of only one instance of this happening in a contemporary marriage, and there the girl's parents were by their own admission very concerned about maintaining appearances so as not to lay themselves open to criticism from relatives who lived nearby. At the other extreme are cases where permission is communicated to the man even before the visit is made.

As informal as such a visit has now become, it is not omitted unless there is some unusual circumstance, such as the woman's parents living far away. It marks the beginning of interfamily relations in contemporary ren'ai marriages, to be followed at some point by a meeting between the two sets of parents. The couple need not be present at this meeting, since the purpose is to begin to establish the rapport and communication at the parental level that would already exist to some extent in miai marriages.

Choosing the Nakōdo

The agreement to have a wedding immediately confronts the couple and their families with a series of decisions that continues up to the wedding day itself. Although the issues are essentially the same for both ren'ai and miai marriages, they tend to be settled in slightly different ways.

In miai marriages events are likely to proceed quickly from the time both parties agree to the match up to the very day of the wedding. There are two reasons for this. First, the two families have usually already met through the mediator, whose good offices help the subsequent decision-making process go more swiftly. The second reason is attitudinal. Put simply, it is considered best to have the couple marry before there is any chance for the relationship to turn sour, a notion summed up by the saying "a springtime that lasts too long may come to naught" (*nagasugita haru wa ikenai*). Although people often use this expression in reference to premarital relationships in general, it is considered particularly relevant in miai marriages because the decision to wed is based largely on first impressions, increasing the likelihood that close interaction between the principals will lead to unanticipated points of friction and conflict.

Another difference between the two marriage processes is the order in which matters are settled. In miai marriages the question of the ceremonial nakōdo comes up early, because of the presence of the mediator who arranged the initial meeting. If this person is suitable for the role of ceremonial nakōdo and acceptable to both parties, the matter is usually settled at once. Even when someone else is preferred, as often happens, the decision must still be made early so that the mediator may step aside and let the ceremonial nakōdo carry out his duties. Once the nakōdo is selected, the details of the *yuinō* (betrothal ceremony) and the wedding are worked out in that order.[9]

In ren'ai marriages the order of these decisions is less predictable, but generally the selection of the nakōdo comes last. In love matches, with their typically well-established relationships, there is little need for a third party to help settle other matters. The presence of the nakōdo may therefore be unnecessary until the yuinō, when his ceremonial functions begin.

The nakōdo normally oversees this ceremony, at which the groom's family formally presents the bride's with a cash betrothal gift. Later he plays the highly visible role in the wedding described in Chapter 1: together with his wife, he accompanies the bride and groom through most of the activities and opens the reception with a speech formally introducing them to the guests. In theory his duties continue after the wedding, since as the public guarantor for the marriage he is supposed to take an active interest in the couple's well-being and act as conciliator in the event of any serious marital dispute. In practice the nakōdo is almost never called on to play conciliator, because most couples avoid involving a third party in their affairs. Any real involvement he may have with the couple's welfare is more likely to be the result of external circumstances: if the nakōdo is the groom's boss, for example, he will probably take a paternalistic interest in the couple, but otherwise may remain distant and unconcerned.

The initiative for maintaining intimate relations after the wedding, moreover, lies with the principals themselves. They will be careful to bring back a gift for the nakōdo from their honeymoon and to pay respectful visits on the two occasions a year when one is supposed to acknowledge one's debt to various superiors with a small gift.[10] In theory the couple's debt to the nakōdo is never discharged, but people say the rule of thumb is that the formalities should be observed for about three years after the wedding, and then the couple are free to keep up the relationship or let it fade, as they see fit.

Regardless of the nature of the relationship and the prospects for maintaining it in the future, the ceremonial role of the nakōdo at the wedding itself is quite clear, and this determines who is eligible. Together with his wife, the nakōdo symbolizes the successful marriage. He should therefore be someone whose own good social standing and stable married life validate his claim as guarantor for the match, and enable him to lend it respectability by appearing with the couple at the ritual moment in their lives when they too gain the status of married people.

Most commonly, in my research, the nakōdo turned out to be an uncle or a company superior of the bride or groom, two categories that together accounted for about three-fourths of the nakōdo selections I learned about.[11] The decision whether to choose a company superior or a relative is greatly influenced by the couple's job situation, especially that of the groom. A man who works in a family-run enterprise is likely to ask a relative or someone who has a relationship with the family as a whole, not just a personal friend or acquaintance. Takagi Ichirō (Case 5), who works in his family's inn, is a good example; even before he had any prospect of marrying, his mother's younger brother expressed a desire to serve as nakōdo.[12]

Among those employed outside the home, there is a particularly strong likelihood of asking a company superior if the bride and groom work for the same company—like Kobayashi Satoru and Hiroko (Case 4) who, as we have seen, even relied on this common bond in making their decision to marry. Satoru says that when it came time to choose the nakōdo, it was really only a question of which superior to ask. As it turned out, this was no simple matter for Satoru, since his work is not directly supervised by any one person. Unsure about the best person to approach, he consulted someone outside his department, who advised him that the easiest thing to do was to ask the company president, a choice that would offend no one. That choice compounded the tendency for the weddings of co-workers to be heavily company-oriented, since many of the guests on both sides are fellow workers, and the most important guests are likely to be company officers.

Individual cases vary, of course. Another informant, Ōsawa Tsutomu, a sales representative for a large electronics firm, also married a woman in his company. However, both his parents and his wife's live in rural districts, where family concerns remain strong and still dominate the tone of the wedding. The couple decided that the potential conflict between company and family interests was too difficult to resolve and ended up holding separate celebrations, a traditional wedding for relatives only and a subsequent party for company personnel. This decision automatically relegated the choice of the nakōdo to a relative.

FOUR

The Stage and Its Managers

"We do what we can to alleviate the customers' anxiety about the proceedings," remarked Nakahara Hajime, one of the directors at White Crane Palace. "It helps make the wedding a more pleasurable and memorable experience for them."

Nakahara, in his early thirties, had worked at White Crane Palace for five years. Before that he had quit his job with the postal service to take an extended trip abroad. He is somewhat taller than average and his slender frame gives him a slightly awkward appearance, but his expression is always pleasant and his manner cordial. His co-workers regard him as something of an intellectual because of his delight in long and detailed explanations. I found him an ideal informant: an attentive observer always willing to share his thoughts.

Nakahara was reflecting on his role as ritual specialist, explaining how part of a director's difficulty stems from the customers' lack of sophistication. "We're not considered one of the elite establishments in the city, so most of the people who come to us are true middle-class types—not very refined." Unfamiliar with the details of formality, they require patient coaching before, and skillful cueing during, the performance. "We have to coddle them a bit," he complained mildly, "because they don't know all that much about ceremony." Nakahara's comment echoes an image—held by many as a legacy of White Crane Palace's origin in the gojokai system—of the facility as an institution for the masses. But his words also point to the larger process of the ordinary person's alienation from ritual expertise, a process that has accompanied the growth of the commercial wedding industry.

In part this alienation can be explained by the massive migration of rural youth to the cities in the 1950s and 1960s. As the newcomers took jobs and settled down, they tended to establish nuclear households with few if any members of the senior generation who in village society served as the repository for traditional knowledge, including matters of ritual procedure. The vacuum thus created is now partially filled by modern-day etiquette manuals. These enjoy tremendous popularity—Shiotsuki Yaeko's best-seller, *Introduction to Ceremonial Etiquette*, originally published in 1970, was already in its 195th printing by 1982.

But alienation in matters of wedding ritual has also resulted from the commercial industry's promotion of newer and more sumptuous forms of celebration, which require considerable skill and expertise to produce. The popular acceptance of these services has accordingly undercut the ability of ordinary people to conduct a suitable ceremony on their own. The transformation of the wedding into an increasingly elaborate performance has thus sharpened the need for both the wedding hall as its stage and the services of commercial specialists to direct it.

In this chapter I continue my account of the events leading up to the wedding with an examination of White Crane Palace: its facilities, its personnel, and its overall influence in the decisions that shape the actual performance of the wedding. I begin, however, with a description of the yuinō, the betrothal ceremony, in which the wedding industry ordinarily has little or no involvement.[1] The experience nonetheless serves to impress upon many families their need for expert guidance, for it can prove to be a frightening lesson in their own unfamiliarity with ritual procedure.

The Yuinō

The yuinō was once a strictly family-to-family affair, consisting of the transfer of betrothal gifts from the groom's household to that of the bride. But it was not a face-to-face transfer, for marriage fell into the realm of important, and therefore delicate, transactions, in which direct interaction between the parties was traditionally avoided. The nakōdo's role as mediator was thus essential (Embree 1939: 173, 204). He conducted the yuinō in stages. Going first to the prospective groom's house, he received the betrothal gifts and was perhaps joined by an older

relative, who would accompany him as the family's representative. He then went to the bride-to-be's home to deliver the
gifts, for which he was given a receipt. After being feasted by
the bride's family, he returned to the groom's house, where
he presented the receipt and was feasted again. The engaged
couple took no part in the proceedings.

The modern version is much simpler. For one thing, the entire
transaction usually takes place in the woman's home. And for
another, parents represent themselves directly, the need for a
mediator having diminished along with the overall decline in the
strength of the familial perspective. But the yuinō still has the
tone of a family affair. The parents' attendance is obligatory, and
the simplest yuinō ceremonies I heard of were meetings between the two sets of parents alone.[2] Still, the principals are expected to attend. Here, too, they may also present each other
with gifts of their own. The custom derives from the Western
practice of giving an engagement ring, to which the Japanese
have added the notion of exchange. Thus in return for the ring
the groom typically gives his bride, he may receive a watch, a
tiepin, a set of cufflinks, or some similar item from her.[3] Both
normally purchase these gifts with their own funds.

The ceremony itself is straightforward; the following synthesis
of accounts given by informants is even less formal than that prescribed by the most recent books on etiquette. The groom's party
usually consists of the young man, his parents, and the nakōdo.
They arrive at the bride's home and are shown into the room to
be used for the ceremony, where they are allowed a few moments by themselves to get settled and lay out the yuinō gifts.
The bride's parents and usually the bride then enter, and the
nakōdo makes a brief statement about the purpose of the occasion, noting the auspiciousness of the day and stressing his anticipation that the relationship will prove an enduring one. He is
careful to use formal language in general, and especially key
words associated with weddings (such as *ikuhisashiku*, "forever," "everlastingly," etc., to express the notion of permanence). He finishes by presenting the gifts to the bride or her
parents, and the bride's father briefly acknowledges receipt of
the goods. The gifts are then transferred to the *tokonoma*—the
decorative alcove traditionally located in the most formal room
of a home—or to an adjoining room. The bride's father will give

the groom's party a formal receipt, either now or sometime later before they leave. After these proceedings, food and drink are brought in and shared by the two parties, and the remainder of the gathering is given over to casual talk and perhaps some discussion of the details of the wedding, all in a more relaxed atmosphere. When the groom and his party leave, the nakōdo usually accompanies them back to their home, where he receives further refreshments and a small cash gift in return for the day's services.

Despite the simplicity of the yuinō in its contemporary form, there is considerable apprehension before, and tension during, the formal part of the ceremony. One reason may be confusion and uncertainty about proper procedure. For many families this is the first experience with the ceremony, and the etiquette books they rely on may be inadequate for the particular situation. In other instances the tension stems rather from personal incompatibility with the kind of formal behavior expected, although the underlying cause may be the same: the selection of someone as nakōdo for reasons other than his skill or experience in the role. The following two examples illustrate.

The first involves Satō Fumio, the young man whose miai experience was described in Chapter 3 (Case 1). Fumio chose as nakōdo a friend of his elder brother, a man who works in Fumio's company and was in fact responsible for his getting a job there. At the time of the ceremony his fiancée's parents were having repairs done to their home, so they rented a room in a nearby restaurant for the yuinō. When Fumio's party, consisting of himself, his parents, and the nakōdo, arrived there, they were shown in and allowed time to get settled and arrange the gifts. Since the nakōdo had never served in that role before, he had prepared by cramming from an etiquette manual, from which he learned they were supposed to seat themselves in a certain orientation toward the tokonoma. He and the other members of the party were therefore at a loss when they entered the room and found it had none. After a bit of discussion, they decided to proceed as though there were a tokonoma in such and such a location, but before they could get fully ready, the bride's party entered. Caught off guard, they ended up sitting just opposite from the place they had settled on as the appropriate one.

The informant in my other example, Ishibashi Osamu, selected as his nakōdo a man who had helped look after Osamu's family from the time he lost his father at age eleven. Osamu and his mother went with this man and his wife to the bride's house for the yuinō, where they were shown into the room for the ceremony. They seated themselves in the proper position in front of the tokonoma and laid the gifts in front of them before the bride's party entered. Osamu described the nakōdo as a very easygoing type, unaccustomed to formalities, but he evidently intended to follow the minimum procedure nonetheless. He had only managed to struggle through the obligatory opening, "Today we are gathered . . . ," however, when his wife burst out laughing at the incongruity of hearing such formal language from her husband's mouth. This broke the man's concentration, and giving up on his resolve to observe protocol, he conducted the rest of the ceremony in an informal and completely unorthodox manner.

Not everyone has as much difficulty with the ceremony, to be sure. Sometimes the nakōdo is a person who enjoys formality and has previous experience in the role. Even then, the situation often generates tension. The yuinō is the initial step in forging a formal relationship between the two families; hence formal recognition of this fact is felt to be appropriate. But the parents, and the nakōdo who represents them, are not yet on familiar terms, particularly in ren'ai marriages in which the yuinō is often only the families' second or even their first meeting. They are thus placed in the uncomfortable situation of having to interact in a serious matter with people who are still very much strangers, and in roles to which they are often unaccustomed.

This point is hardly lost on the wedding industry. "The *yuinō* can be plagued by a surprising number of problems," declares a White Crane Palace advertisement for a recently instituted service. Customers are invited to avoid "the anxiety over intricate formalities and providing the proper gifts, food, and drinks" by using the hall's facilities in lieu of their homes for the yuinō. The wedding hall will even provide personnel to direct the proceedings. The service has yet to gain much popularity, however, despite the promise of "peace of mind at an outstanding value" and offers of discounts to Gojokai members.

The one service the wedding hall does provide for many customers in connection with the yuinō is furnishing the gifts—or more accurately, a set of ceremonial items in which the main gift of cash is included for formal presentation. These items derive from the yuinō customs of the Tokugawa period, when the betrothal payment consisted primarily of cloth, clothing, food, and drink (Ema 1971: 138). Later it became common to substitute cash for the cloth and articles of clothing, the most important of the items given. But an array of traditional gifts has been retained, largely for their symbolic meanings. Some items symbolize reproduction and fertility, such as a dried cuttlefish of a phallic shape; or a piece of seaweed whose name, *konbu*, is represented in the ceremony with characters meaning "child-bearing woman"; or a pair of fish, male and female, placed together belly to belly. Other items are symbolic of the hoped-for longevity of the match, such as a long hempen cord, which is likened to the couple's hair grown white with age, or a folding fan, said by its spreading shape to denote the marriage's increasing prosperity and/or future issue.[4]

Such items are wrapped in distinctive envelopes of a type commonly used for formal gifts. White Crane Palace provides them in sets to Gojokai members at no charge; nonmembers purchase them for prices ranging from ¥12,000 to ¥20,000, depending on which items are included. They are rarely dispensed with, although many people are not very particular about them. It is not unheard of for families to use sets they received at the betrothal of a sibling, for example. This describes the attitude of most toward the formality associated with the yuinō: proper procedure is felt to be necessary, but few express enthusiasm for it.

The main item given is the cash payment. Normally the man's parents supply most or all of the money, which is typically received by the woman's parents rather than the woman herself. A rule of thumb sets the payment at roughly three times the prospective groom's monthly salary, although most people in Hirayama now consider ¥500,000 ($2,083)—a higher amount for most men—the standard figure.[5] Although some men are spendthrifts who have not managed to save any money by the time they marry, and others working in family enterprises cannot differentiate personal earnings from family funds, most have at least this much in their own savings accounts. Even so, the grooms-to-be, as well as their parents, still see the yuinō as a family-to-family transaction, and are content to let their parents make the payment while they reserve their own funds for other, personal goals.

Scheduling the Wedding

While the yuinō remains largely an interaction between two families—despite the wedding industry's attempts to colonize it—other matters to be decided before the wedding increasingly involve the participation of commercial specialists. Even setting the date for the wedding requires a visit to one or more establishments to check the availability of the facilities.

By then, however, most considerations that go into scheduling the wedding have been taken into account. Often the date, or a series of desirable dates, is decided in conjunction with the timing of the yuinō. Most people hold that the bridal payment should be used to purchase the things the woman will take to her new home—clothes, kitchen utensils and appliances, furniture, and the like. It is preferable, then, to have the yuinō from two months to as much as half a year before the wedding, to give the bride and her family time to make proper preparations.

Another general consideration has to do with the season. The preferred time is spring or fall, and there is a particularly strong aversion to the hot late-summer months of July and August, because the dress code calls for roughly the same degree of formality regardless of season.[6] To a lesser degree the winter months of December and January are also avoided, partly because of a preference for more temperate weather, and partly because of conflicts with other ceremonial events. The New Year is the most important holiday in Japan, and it generates a flurry of activity in the weeks preceding and following the first of January. There are other seasonal considerations, such as the work schedules of the families or other people expected to attend. Weddings tend not to be scheduled during the region's busiest agricultural seasons, for example.

Once the approximate time for the wedding has been decided, the determination of the precise day depends largely on the *koyomi*, the astrological calendar. The literal meaning of koyomi is simply "calendar," but the term normally refers specifically to the system of lunar months used before the adoption of the Western calendar in 1872. The latter is now used in almost all aspects of daily life. The koyomi has been relegated to a small number of special roles connected mostly with choosing days for such ceremonial events as weddings and funerals, and for a few other momentous occasions, such as the groundbreaking for a new house or even the purchase of a new car. There are a number of ways in which the koyomi can be used for such reckoning; the one most commonly employed relies on a six-day sequence of astrological labels designating each day as suitable or unsuitable for certain types of events.[7]

Leisure time is determined by the work week, and Sunday is the day off for most Japanese. As important as the marriage process is held to be, the wedding is usually scheduled for a Sunday or a holiday so that as many guests as possible may attend. But synchronizing the work calendar with the six-day astrological sequence greatly complicates things. Two of the six designations—Taian and Tomobiki—are considered the most auspicious for matters related to weddings. They are preferred for the yuinō as well as for the wedding itself, if either falls on a Sunday or other day convenient for most of those expected to attend. One designation—Butsumetsu—is inauspicious enough to be consistently avoided, even if it falls on a day that by all other criteria is most suitable for everyone concerned.

Since relatively few Sundays or holidays coincide with either Taian or Tomobiki, the range of preferred days, in the preferred season, is narrow indeed. Almanacs (also called koyomi) that relate the six-day astrological sequence to the seven-day week must be consulted to determine whether any particular day is considered good or bad.[8] Should no astrologically preferred day coincide with a holiday in the general time period, any convenient Sunday or holiday that is not labeled Butsumetsu is likely to be chosen. The three remaining designations are nowadays considered neutral with regard to weddings and are therefore acceptable. Indeed, most people take a fairly relaxed attitude toward the entire matter, with very little commitment on the part of the participants to these beliefs. Many young people in particular say that it does not matter to them whether the wedding is on a Taian day or not, or that they would just as soon have it on one designated Butsumetsu. They go along with the custom because it might upset others if they appeared to be flouting it, especially if the wedding will be attended by older relatives or those living in rural areas—people who are felt to put more stock in such superstitions.

The principals are often more concerned with how astrological considerations will affect the availability of wedding facilities. Because of the overwhelming preference for Sundays and holidays and especially for those that coincide with astrologically preferred designations, a premium is placed on the dozen or so such days that normally occur during each of the two busy seasons of the year.[9] Commercial establishments are flooded well in advance with applications for these days, so that it is sometimes difficult or impossible to get a reservation for the time and place one wants. Two examples related by informants illustrate the kinds of complexities that can attend the process of selecting a specific day for the wedding.

Ōta Toshinori and Yoshie, whose informal miai was described in Chapter 3 (Case 2), made their decision to marry within several weeks of their first meeting in early July. Their families held a yuinō ceremony on September 13, selected because it was an auspicious day according to the koyomi. It was suggested at the yuinō that the following spring would be a good time for the wedding. After a bit of reflection, Yoshie's mother objected on the grounds that Yoshie's younger brother was planning to enter a university that April. Both he, and to some extent other family members, would be busy in February and March with preparations for the entrance examinations, and once he began school, the family would have an added financial burden as well. The families agreed therefore to hold the ceremony in late January or early February. November and December were ruled out primarily because this would not leave sufficient time for the necessary preparations, but the parties also felt that it would be difficult to get a reservation during the busier fall season. When Toshinori and Yoshie went to inquire at the establishment they selected, however, they were surprised to find that their first preference in late January was already crowded, so that the only times available were either too early or too late in the day for their liking. Their first choice had been a Taian Sunday, hence a particularly good day; they settled for the following Sunday, which was designated Senshō and therefore astrologically neutral.

The case of Yoshida Minoru, thirty, and Kuniko, twenty-nine, resembles that of the Ōtas in the sense that their marriage too began with an informal introduction from someone roughly their own age. Neither of them had asked this man, Kuniko's friend and Minoru's cousin, to look for a suitable partner for them, but he had been aware that both were approaching thirty without any immediate prospect of marrying and felt their personalities were so compatible that chances for a match were good. On his own initiative, he suggested an introduction to each separately, and they all agreed to meet one Saturday at a coffee shop downtown. The Yoshidas describe the meeting as more like a gathering of friends, and quite unlike a formal miai, the more so since their parents were not present (although Minoru's aunt—the cousin's mother—had come along "just to go shopping"). Within three months, Minoru and Kuniko decided to marry, and they soon secured the consent of their parents. The yuinō took place shortly afterward, in early April.

Even before the yuinō, both sides had agreed to an early-fall wedding and had also decided on a place for the ceremony. They chose a popular Shinto shrine near Minoru's house, his preference because of its location and because his sister and several relatives had been married there. After making an initial inquiry about the shrine's availability (along with that of a nearby wedding hall for the reception), Minoru and Kuniko came to the yuinō with a list of possible dates. The two parties decided on October 10, a Senshō Sunday and a national holiday (Physical Education Day—with the following Monday being celebrated as a public holiday in its place). The final selection was based on four considerations: (1) it came during an agricultural off-season for Kuniko's parents and other relatives, who are farmers; (2) it was before the beginning of the heavy tourist season for Minoru's relatives, who run a hotel in a scenic mountain district; (3) it was during an extended holiday, making it easier for other relatives who had to come from farther away; and (4) it was astrologically acceptable.

Choosing the Place

Many couples follow the Yoshidas' example of choosing an establishment on the basis of prior experience there, although it is usually considerations about the reception, rather than the ceremony, that prove critical. Satō Fumio (Case 1) and his wife selected a wedding hall where they had both been favorably impressed with the receptions they had recently attended. Sometimes, though, the couple's impressions count less than those of their parents. This was doubtless more frequent in the prewar period, when the parents almost always selected the establishment. Seasoned wedding hall personnel report that it was still common in the early 1970s for the parents to make the first inquiry about schedules and costs. Nowadays the couple usually do this themselves.

Parents may still have strong preferences, though perhaps out of an awareness of changing mores, these may not be expressed immediately. This was the experience of Nakamura Takashi, who like most grooms-to-be had been told by his parents that he and his fiancée should find a suitable place for the wedding on their own. Takashi was very concerned about costs, since he neither sought nor anticipated any support from his parents, who have always had to live on very modest means. As a public school teacher, he himself has only managed to maintain a precarious state of financial independence since he graduated from college. After quickly investigating several places, he and his fiancée decided to have the wedding at a municipally run facility at which he, as a civil servant, would get a special discount. When they informed her family of this decision, it turned out that her parents had preferred another establishment all along, a place that had impressed them when they served as nakōdo there. Takashi realized then that none of his wishes for a simple wedding would be recognized by his fiancée's family, but decided that letting her parents have their way was a small price to pay for their willing consent to the match.

Concern about costs is especially acute in cases like the Nakamuras, in which the couple bear a considerable part of the expense. Such couples predictably opt for low-cost establishments when they do get their way. Urata Kanji and Asami paid all the costs associated with their marriage, for example, and this enabled them to have a rather unorthodox wedding. The ceremony was held at a church in Hawaii and not attended by any friends or family.[10] Asami points out the financial advantage of this: the couple had intended to go to Hawaii for their honeymoon regardless, the wedding service itself was cheap, and the rental of a bridal dress and tuxedo for the occasion cost only ¥30,000. On their return they had a reception at an ordinary restaurant—not one of the city's *ryōtei* (traditional-style restaurant) that had provided such services in the past, but a modern establishment that had never before been asked to host a wedding reception. The couple paid considerably less than the cost of a reception provided by the wedding industry. Their parents had no part in planning either the ceremony or the reception. Kanji's willingness to become an in-marrying husband partly explains this; Asami's parents would have been reluctant to make strong demands of someone who consented to such a generally unattractive arrangement. It may also explain the couple's desire to give their wedding such an independent flavor.

At the other extreme are cases in which the parents use economic leverage to turn the wedding into a statement about the status of the family as a whole. When Suzuki Ken'ichi and Tomoko agreed to marry, for example, they decided that a wedding hall near Hirayama Station would be most convenient. The couple work for a company located in Hirayama, but live in towns lying in opposite directions from it along the same railway line, so they reasoned that the easiest thing to do was to have both sets of relatives and hometown friends take the train and meet in the center; this was also convenient for those guests from their company who make Hirayama their home.

There are several establishments near the station; their wedding was held in the most prestigious of them, one of the three or four places that fall in the first-class group of the local wedding industry. The selection of this site reflects the concern of the groom's father, who is president of his own company, to make an impression on the many guests he wanted to invite. Most of these were his business associates. Ken'ichi comments that at times he had little sense of it being his own wedding; his position as chōnan no doubt made it harder for him to distinguish personal interests from those of his family. But he did not protest either the wedding's scale or the lavish expenditure on it, since his father was paying all of his family's share of the costs, and Ken'ichi was able to invite his own guests.

In other cases more specific connections with a particular establishment motivate its selection. Ōta Toshihiko (Case 2) selected a certain wedding hall because his aunt worked there, and this he felt was an assurance of receiving good service. Besides, his family had become members of the gojokai plan connected with that establishment long before he had reached the tekireiki, in anticipation of his eventual marriage.

A Backstage Look at White Crane Palace

Choosing a commercial establishment is but the first of many decisions the couple and their parents must make in consultation with the firm's personnel. Even though the amalgamation of services that has accompanied the industry's growth provides the convenience of dealing with a single organization, there are still many decisions to be made. At White Crane Palace it takes at least six or seven visits to complete all the necessary arrangements.

A tour of White Crane Palace gives an indication of the variety of services it now regularly provides. When customers arrive at the modern two-story building, they enter through the main doors to face a front desk, where an employee refers them to the proper department for specific services. Off to the side is a large lobby, crowded on busy days with guests waiting for a wedding or a reception to begin. There is a counter at one end of the lobby where customers and guests can purchase coffee and other refreshments at regular restaurant prices. Another large area is taken up by the clothing-rental department, with separate rooms for hairdressing as well as for fitting brides in their wedding costumes. Grooms are also provided with formal wedding clothes here.

The middle of the first floor houses the department in charge of reservations and requests for wedding-related services. It has a long counter where employees consult with customers about upcoming weddings, and the area in front has tables and chairs for those who must wait their turn at the counter, as frequently happens on busy days. Behind this waiting area stand row upon row of glass cases with samples of the items available as hikidemono, the presents that the wedding guests are given to take home as souvenirs of the event. White Crane Palace obtains these items from outside suppliers on its customers' behalf. In

addition to the household articles such as kitchenware, table-
ware, clocks, and linens that are commonly selected as hikidemono, some kind of edible item is usually given. Samples or
representations of these are also exhibited in the glass cases. In
this area there is also a separate counter staffed by a travel
agency, which makes arrangements for the honeymoon. The
rest of the first floor is taken up by the kitchen, which prepares
most of the food for the wedding reception.

The second floor has two main sets of rooms: the wedding
area, with three waiting rooms for the wedding party and the
shrine room where the ceremony takes place; and the reception
area, with eight ballrooms and an adjoining large space where
the waiters and waitresses handle the food and other items
brought in and out of the reception. In addition, there are two
photographic studios where the formal pictures of the newlyweds and the wedding party are taken.

Customer Interaction

A simple inquiry about costs and the availability of facilities
does not mean that a couple have made a given establishment
their firm choice, so at the initial encounter the personnel of
White Crane Palace make a particular point of stressing the ad-
vantages of having a wedding there. The strategy followed is
frequently the same one the wedding hall uses in its attempts to
lure new business: exploiting the fact that it is the young people
who now usually select the place for the wedding, White Crane
Palace focuses on what is likely to interest them most. Its advertisements feature the honeymoon plans it makes available at discount rates, for example, since like the Uratas (above), couples
may be thinking about their honeymoon more than the quality
of the service. Because many also worry more about costs than
their parents do, honeymoon plans are combined with special
discounts on wedding services as well.

This strategy was clearly visible in an encounter I observed between Kawano Gorō, the head of the reservation department,
and a couple who had come to make an initial inquiry. Kawano
asked them the approximate date of the wedding and where
they planned to go for their honeymoon, which turned out to be
Hawaii. He handed them a packet on White Crane Palace's ser-

vices and costs, calling their attention to a plan that gives special discounts for weddings held on days other than Sundays, holidays, and Taian Saturdays. If they picked an ordinary Saturday, he explained, they could save approximately ¥20,000 ($833) on the honeymoon, ¥120,000 ($500) on the bridal robes, and ¥93,000 ($387) on the reception, and still choose a more elaborate bill of fare than normally provided. Kawano stressed the advantages of an ordinary Saturday, arguing that guests usually had little difficulty taking a Saturday off for a wedding, so it was virtually as convenient as a Sunday. Moreover, the wedding hall was not as crowded on that day, so the couple could enjoy a leisurely reception, whereas on busy Sundays they faced a two-hour limit. He also recommended that they join the Gojokai, since the wedding would take place after the minimum 180-day membership period making them eligible for benefits. Kawano explained the financial advantages of membership, emphasizing that if the couple combined this with a wedding on an ordinary Saturday they would be saving a considerable amount. At the close of the session, he gave them two tickets redeemable at the coffee counter, stating that since they had taken the trouble to come, they should relax and have a leisurely cup before they left.

Afterward Kawano explained to me that since the couple did not have any prior commitment to White Crane Palace, they would probably compare other places before making their decision, so he considered it important to recommend the cheapest plan possible. He also pointed out the advantage to White Crane Palace when such parties decide to have a wedding on an ordinary day, since the more popular days are certain to fill up regardless and the Palace would have to turn people away. Hence the special discount plans serve a double purpose.

Subsequent meetings between customers and staff involve the selection of specific items and services from among alternatives offered by the wedding hall. Many selections are made on the same occasion, at one of the special bridal exhibits White Crane Palace puts on several times each year to simplify the process. Each exhibit is scheduled for two or three days when the wedding hall is not busy. Customers with reservations for weddings in the near future are invited to attend. During the exhibit the second floor is converted into a showroom, with personnel from the appropriate departments explaining the choices available. Customers pick up order forms at the front desk as they enter the building and are directed to the first display, of bridal robes, in one of the larger rooms upstairs. After making a selection, or in some cases simply viewing the range of possibilities while deferring a final decision, customers are sent to the next exhibit, until they have made their way through all of the displays and back to the reservation department on the first floor.[11]

Although the couple usually come alone for the initial inquiry, almost all parties at the exhibits include at least one parent and quite often one or both parents on each side. The parents' participation is understandable, given that they often pay most or all of the wedding costs and thus have an interest in deciding how the money is to be spent. Differences of opinion may arise, typically over the couple's preference for less expensive choices, and the parents' preference for costlier ones. In one group the groom-to-be and his mother carried on a lively exchange over the merits of a twelve- vs. thirteen-dish menu for the reception.[12] The son pointed out that there was very little difference between the two (in fact, the difference is the addition of a stuffed lobster half, which raises the cost by ¥1,200 per guest). His mother countered that they were skimping a bit on the gifts already, and since there would be only forty or so guests at the wedding anyway, they might as well opt for fancier food. The son prevailed, at least for the time being. Meanwhile the girl and her mother, who made up the rest of the group, stood off to the side and took no part in the decision.

More often matters are settled jointly between the two families. This appears particularly true of the selection of the bridal kimono, according to Mrs. Sugita, an employee of the department handling these rentals. Very rarely do the couple decide by themselves; even if they come alone, the woman will usually return later with her mother. Generally both sets of parents accompany the principals and collaborate on the decision. But this does not rule out conflict. Mrs. Sugita related an incident she had recently observed in which the bride chose a particular kimono in the ¥200,000 range, but was argued out of it by the groom's elder sister, who claimed it was simply too expensive. The bride came back later to look at the robe again, saying she really wanted to wear it, but in the end she had to settle for a less costly one. Mrs. Sugita sympathized with her and speculated that the groom's family was perhaps not very pleased with the match, so the bride was not in a good position to make strong demands.

Other Decisions

Printing services connected with the wedding are also regularly handled through White Crane Palace. Orders for invitations go to the printer approximately six weeks before the wedding, so the party must decide well in advance on the style and number they need. It is almost always the couple rather than their parents who select the invitations. They are given a choice of different motifs for the outside and two versions for the wording inside, one extending the invitation in their own names, the other extending it in their parents' names. Almost all couples decide to use their parents' names. The invitations are printed in about a week, when the couple come by to pick them up. They address and send out the invitations themselves. R.S.V.P.s are obligatory.

Three weeks before the date of the wedding, the principals inform White Crane Palace of the precise number of guests. They also decide at this time on the seating arrangement for the reception, so that seating charts can be ordered. These note each person's name, seating position, and relation to the bride or groom. Members of the immediate family, relatives, friends, or neighbors of the principals are identified as such; all other guests are designated *raihin* ("visitor"), a term that may be applied to company superiors or business associates, former teachers, friends of the parents, and so forth. The basic outline for the seating arrangement is everywhere the same. The newlyweds, together with the nakōdo and his wife, sit in the traditional place of honor at the far end of the room from the entrance. The parents, as the hosts who have invited everyone else, occupy the least prestigious positions at the corners of the room farthest from the couple's table; the groom's and bride's parties take the right and left halves of the room, respectively, as seen from the couple's table, and the more important guests are seated closest to the couple.

At the reservation department customers fill out order forms with the seating arrangement they have chosen. Occasionally there are differences between the customers' preference and the standards that White Crane Palace believes should apply. These do not arise over the principle of hierarchy as such, but turn instead on which categories of people should occupy the higher ranked seats. The forms provided by White Crane Palace state explicitly that the order is raihin, friends, neighbors, relatives, members of parents' collateral families, members of the principals' families. According to Kōno Shizuko, one of the employees in the reservation department, when customers have a different preference, it is usually because the parents want to put a relative in the most important position. White Crane Palace tries to get them to conform to its pattern, particularly if the raihin include the principals' and especially the groom's company personnel. Kōno claims they are trying to spare the customer the embarrassment of unknowingly flouting convention; but White Crane Palace's own reputation also might suffer if it allowed its customers to offend their guests.

Just before the wedding, ordinarily about a week ahead of time, a final meeting is held to plan the format of the reception. It is usually attended only by the couple and the person they have selected to act as emcee, though occasionally a parent or sibling will sit in. Here they meet with the director of their reception, who explains White Crane Palace's standard format and asks if they wish to alter it in any way. Customers may decide on the inclusion or deletion of certain services at this point or change the order of some of the events. Sometimes they also decide to include events not provided by White Crane Palace, particularly if the emcee is experienced or innovative enough to organize activities on his own.[13]

The emcee in most cases is a friend of the groom selected because of his experience in the role or his ability as a public speaker. If none of the groom's friends is appropriate or willing to serve, White Crane Palace can supply the emcee. One employee told me they prefer to do so because of the importance of the role. He always warns customers that in his estimation 90 percent of the reception's success depends on the emcee's performance, so they are well advised to use one of White Crane Palace's experienced men if they do not know anyone who is really dependable. Some concern for direct economic return may be behind his recommendation, for White Crane Palace collects a fee of ¥20,000 ($83) for providing the emcee. But the wedding hall places considerable emphasis on the quality of the emcee's performance regardless of how he is chosen, and provides the couple's choice with models and guidelines. He is given a book, for example, containing samples of lines suitable for introducing the various speakers and events. Many emcees follow these samples to the letter, compiling them into a script to read during the reception, although some include variations or insert new lines of their own. Much of the planning session may be given over to coaching a novice emcee with advice about what to do and what blunders to avoid.

The remainder of the session concerns various logistical matters. The director makes certain the couple and the emcee have selected the people they wish to give speeches or other performances, and advises them to get the candidates' consent as soon as possible, if they have not done so, to avoid last-minute problems and misunderstandings. He also has the couple select the music to be played for their entrances and exits and during the cake-cutting ceremony and other events. Most choose from the range of standard choices White Crane Palace offers, but customers are encouraged to substitute some particular favorite or a song that might be especially meaningful to the guests, as a way of giving the reception a more individual flavor.

The Ritual Specialist: Goals and Strategies

The dialogue between children and parents that began with the decision to marry thus ends as the final details of the wedding are settled. It is a dialogue often punctuated by conflicts, which the director—increasingly an intermediary in the dialogue—tries both to resolve and to exploit for his own purposes. I now examine more closely the conflict between parents and children as one of the several contradictions the personnel of White Crane Palace must confront in the pursuit of their goals as ritual specialists.

Conflicts and Contradictions

Parents are typically more concerned about how a wedding will reflect on the family as a whole; the couple usually want to

make a more individual statement. The first concern faces outward: parents worry about what others might say, about how
the wedding will measure up to current standards. Their children's interests address the event itself: they want it to be a celebration, a sharing of their joy with those who really care.

The case of Nakamura Takashi introduced above best illustrates these tendencies, because his financial independence
from his parents had enabled him to define his own goals clearly.
He personally conducted most of the negotiations leading to his
marriage, culminating a three-year courtship that sprang from
an informal introduction by a mutual friend. Takashi's parents,
who live a half-day's journey from Hirayama, came in for the
yuinō and of course the wedding but were otherwise not involved. Takashi had wanted to dispense with the wedding ceremony entirely and have a simple party-type reception given
over entirely to celebration, without any of the usual trappings
such as a wedding cake. He abandoned these hopes when the
conflict over the wedding site revealed that his future parents-
in-law had definite desires about the ceremony's size and shape.
He characterizes their ideas as ostentatious, the product of their
age and rural background. Older people in his wife's area—in
the mountains well north of Hirayama—pay a lot of attention to
the hikidemono, according to Takashi. The first thing they do
when they get home after a wedding is open the gift and ap-
praise it as either a fine piece of merchandise or just so-so, trying
to figure out how much the principals' families paid for it and
how much they laid out for the entire wedding. Young people
are more interested in just having a good time.

Sometimes the parents are less concerned with making a good
impression on others than with simply keeping up the proper
appearances. Kobayashi Satoru and his wife Hiroko (Case 4,
Chap. 3) share Takashi's dislike of formal ceremony. Their selection of their company president as nakōdo made it imperative
that they observe protocol; their decision to have the wedding in
one of the city's elite establishments was a direct result. The
couple claim that they managed nonetheless to have things close
to the way they wanted, and feel it was really their wedding and
not something done by and for their families. Satoru notes that
they sent out the invitations in their own names, contrary to
custom. Hiroko adds that they were probably able to do so be-

cause of their ages (thirty-three and twenty-nine at the time of their marriage); had they been in their early twenties this would have been impossible. They had also eliminated many of the standard features of the commercialized wedding, which they thought inane. But they kept the cake-cutting because Hiroko's mother insisted that it would not seem like a wedding without one.

Sometimes there is no conflict at all. Parents may be quite willing to let their children have everything their way, as in the case of the Uratas, the couple who married in Hawaii. Or parental desire to maintain appearances may be motivated less by a concern over the family's image than by a concern for the children's happiness—and many young couples are indeed quite happy to make this once-in-a-lifetime occasion an extravagant one. Like the bride who wanted to wear the expensive kimono, they may have no qualms about the sumptuousness of the standard commercial wedding, as long as finances permit.

Where conflict does arise, finances indeed often decide the issue. To the principals' complaint, "It's too extravagant," the parents may counter, "We'll pay for it." Few couples have the resources and determination to follow the Uratas' example and take care of everything by themselves; the amount of money involved forces most to rely on their parents. The extent to which they do so varies greatly, but the following pattern held true for my informants. The principals use whatever financial resources they have to cover expenses reflecting individual rather than familial concerns. A man pays for the engagement ring and honeymoon if he has any money at all, and also takes care of some of the expense involved in setting up the postmarital residence. If after meeting these costs, he still has some savings, he may provide part or all of the yuinō payment and contribute to the cost of the wedding. A woman pays first of all for the return engagement gift, then for the furniture and other items she will take to her new residence, before trying to help with her side's share of the wedding costs.[14]

Wedding industry personnel are of course aware that children and parents are likely to differ in their perspectives. They show considerable skill in exploiting the difference, in fact; recall the strategy of appealing to the young people's interests with honeymoon packages and the like to attract new business. But the wedding industry is also keenly aware that it is the parents who ordinarily meet most of the expense. Indeed, the gojokai system relies on parental concerns over wedding costs to boost enrollments, often long before any children are even thinking about marriage. The industry is careful, moreover, to represent the wedding as a family affair at certain critical moments. The director, in his announcements and instructions on the wedding day, when all the guests are present, always takes care to use only the couple's surnames, referring to the event with phrases like "the wedding of the Uchiyama and Okamoto households." But the commercial specialist's overall aim is to balance the differing concerns of all the participants, guests and customers alike. He will advise couples to try and get as many of the guests as possible involved in the speeches and songs during the reception, for example, to prevent any particular group from feeling left out—a danger especially when both bride and groom work for the same company, and ties formed by the workplace dominate the proceedings.

For that matter, the specialist's balancing act may have more to do with the conflicting or even contradictory goals of his firm than with those of his clients. At White Crane Palace such a tension has existed ever since the Gojokai began to respond to competition with the promise that it could deliver better ceremonies for less. On the one hand this promise has prompted the company to try to provide a more sumptuous atmosphere, more attentive service, and more elegant food than it once did. On the other the company now has a double incentive to keep costs down, for it must strive to keep the price of its services low enough to be attractive to customers, yet still make a profit. The contradiction between the goals of sumptuous appearance and economy leads to frequent differences of opinion between the business office and those involved in the actual provision of services. I occasionally heard the directors grumble about what they saw as the business office's stingy attitude. "Why do they keep buying tangerines so late in the season?" Served as dessert, tangerines are considered a treat in September when few have come to market and they are expensive. By November they are plentiful and cheap; White Crane Palace continues to serve them in mid-December. At other times the fare differed, but the complaint was the same: "Why can't they make the slices of melon a bit thicker?"

The problem posed by the conflicting goals of service and profit is not unique to White Crane Palace, to be sure. It is one that every establishment in the service industry faces, including the wedding hall's suppliers. One of the waitresses, for example, told me about a complaint received from Fuji Restaurant, which is called in to satisfy the occasional customer who wants sushi included in the banquet. Fuji's chefs sometimes come to the hall to prepare individual servings on small lacquer plates provided by the restaurant. The plates are not the best grade lacquerware—a quick look reveals that the simple gold-leaf design is applied with a stamp rather than a brush—but they are expensive enough for Fuji to be concerned about their returning in the same numbers that were sent out. When one turned up missing, the restaurant promptly informed White Crane Palace and asked what the wedding hall was willing to do about it. There is little doubt that a guest had walked off with it; White Crane Palace finds that its own dishes constantly get slipped in among the presents and leftovers, the guests' legitimate take-home items. Another waitress's comments about Fuji's complaint reflect White Crane Palace's resignation to the problem: "What they ought to do, you know, is stop using such expensive plates. They can switch to plastic ones, and then they wouldn't have to fret so much." White Crane Palace had recently made such a switch. But the plastic dish it introduced was so cheap looking that it had prompted derisive comments even from the waitresses. The dilemma both sushi restaurants and wedding halls must face is that such attempts to reduce expenses threaten their image of luxury. The strategy set by White Crane Palace's business office frequently overrides considerations of appearance for those of cost, to the displeasure of the directors.

Motivations

Even if the goal of providing service is contradicted by other concerns at White Crane Palace, it is one that is genuinely held by most of the personnel. One long-time employee, proudly emphasizing White Crane Palace's superior service, was sharply critical of the competition:

Why should the Grand Hotel be considered first class all of a sudden, after all the years of experience we've had at providing weddings? It wasn't built as a wedding hall; none of them [the other elite establishments] were. Sometimes when I pass by the entrance I'm amazed at how narrow and dark it is—not a very pleasant setting for a wedding. And Gold Pavilion Inn—its rooms weren't designed for receptions, really. They're too small; they've got you squeezed in there with no space between your back and the wall behind you. It made me so mad the time I was invited to a wedding there! It's only called first class because people think it's first class, so they're willing to pay more for less.

The directors in particular are strongly motivated by the goal of service. All expressed their wish to do something for the customer he cannot do for himself, to make his experience easier and more pleasurable, to make it a memorable wedding. But they tend to vary in the relative emphasis they give different aspects of their role, leading to striking differences in style. Shimomura Takakazu, in his early twenties one of the youngest directors, is particularly energetic in displaying the spirit of service by clearly indicating his customers' elevated status. During a reception he will frequently run from one end of the room to the other to show a speaker to the microphone, or to lead the newlyweds or somebody else to their places. He may finish up with a flashy pose, falling to one knee to hand a microphone up to the speaker, or making an exaggerated bow, arm fully extended, as he guides the newlyweds from one place to another.

By contrast Nakahara Hajime, whom we met at the beginning of this chapter, once warned me never to run in front of the guests, since that would only exacerbate whatever anxieties people might have about the proceedings. Even when Nakahara gets caught too far away to show a speaker or the couple to their places on time, he feels it is important to the success of the reception for the director to avoid giving the impression that something is amiss. In such cases the person can usually figure out what to do on his own, and the director fulfills his role of helping the guests remain calm by not getting excited himself. For this reason, too, Nakahara prefers not to plan out the details of the reception too closely beforehand. A well-planned performance may indeed be more successful in ways, but if something goes wrong it leaves everyone—participants and personnel alike—at a loss for what to do, creating a bad impression. Better to build a certain degree of flexibility into the performance from the beginning, he feels, than to rely too much on detailed planning.

Others disagree, among them Ueda Eiji, a mature man of around forty, who puts greatest emphasis on making the wedding a moving, and therefore memorable, occasion. When working with the couple and the emcee before the wedding, he helps them plan each event in meticulous detail, seeking the combination of elements that will yield the maximum emotional effect. He frequently experiments with new forms, suggesting different texts for the narration or themes for the emcee to emphasize in his introductions and comments. Ueda also tries new ways of dramatizing entrances, exits, and poses through complex manipulations of lights and music, which he carefully rehearses to assure a smooth performance.

All these emphases are visible in the pattern of services that characterizes the commercialized wedding. Through those services the director is able to provide his customers with an experience they could not achieve by themselves. He and the other personnel also maintain a reassuring presence, giving cues at critical moments for customers who often "don't know all that much about ceremony" and thus feel anxious about unfamiliar proceedings. Finally, through the elaborately staged events he directs he helps the principals star in a romantic and sumptuous performance—the "storybook ceremony of love" promised by the wedding hall's brochure.

But these concerns hardly provide an exhaustive explanation of the contemporary wedding—in fact, they barely hint at the symbolic content that differentiates it from other ceremonies and banquets. In the next chapter I begin my examination of this content, which I argue must be understood as a ritual that at once celebrates the transition of the bride and groom into the status of husband and wife and portrays the basic values of society. For it is the portrayal of these values—not the thickness of the slice of melon or the quality of the service—that makes the gathering a wedding.

FIVE

Imaging the Marital Ideal

Rites of passage have long been known to share a common structure, in which the transition from the old status to the new is never abrupt but instead occurs in stages (Turner 1967; Van Gennep 1960). The person making the transition is first shown as separated from his former status. In classic anthropological examples, this is often accomplished by a period of actual seclusion from the rest of society—although the same effect may be achieved through a symbolic marking of separateness, as we shall see for the wedding. Later on, the ritual subject emerges from this separate state, thereby signaling the attainment of his new status. Henceforth he will be "expected to behave in accordance with . . . customary norms and ethical standards" appropriate to that status (Turner 1967: 94).

It is during the liminal phase, the stage of separation, that symbolism is typically richest, and it is indeed here in the wedding that we find the subject matter of our analysis: a symbolic expression of the marital ideal, in images projected of the roles the principals will assume as husband and wife. One explanation for this symbolism is to see it as part of the instruction characteristic of these rites, instruction believed to enable those making the transition "to undertake successfully the tasks of their new office" by effecting a change in their nature and thus "transform[ing] them from one kind of human being into another" (Turner 1967: 108). But the images found in the wedding are clearly stereotypes, abstractions that may never be realized in everyday life. How, then, could one substantiate the claim that they actually "instruct" or even "transform" the principals, if there always remains a discrepancy between these ideals and their subsequent behavior? Perhaps it is best to see any practical results of such statements as lying more in their ability to shape cognition—rather than behavior—by helping reorient social perceptions of the couple. The association of the bride and groom with ideal images of the roles of husband and wife firmly locates them in their new social identities as married persons in the minds of all the participants, including the principals themselves.[1]

On the other hand, there is a very real sense in which these images do instruct. Although stereotypes, they draw on more fundamental understandings the Japanese share about relations between men and women, about the individual and his place in society, and about the nature of society itself and the shape that social relations therefore ought to take. Accordingly they may indeed serve as a "symbolic template of the whole system of beliefs and values" whose articulation in ritual, Turner claims, teaches participants the proper way to think "about their cultural milieu" and thereby "gives them ultimate standards of reference" (Turner 1967: 108). But these are matters to take up later, after we examine the images of the marital ideal projected in the wedding.

The Shinto Ceremony

I begin where the wedding day itself begins, with the Shinto ceremony, and specifically with its historical development. The most striking consideration, in that connection, is to note that the Shinto ceremony is such a successful blend of ancient and relatively modern elements that many Japanese are surprised when told of its recent origin. I have heard some informants speculate that the rite is more than a thousand years old. In fact it was first performed on May 10, 1900, for the wedding of Crown Prince Yoshihito, the future Emperor Taisho. This was the first imperial wedding since the early years of the Meiji Restoration, the political upheaval that ushered Japan into the modern era in the late 1860s. Behind this ceremonial innovation lay the Meiji government's policy of using the imperial institution as a symbol for the new order. Reversing the centuries-old pattern by which emperors had lived in complete isolation from their subjects, the Meiji leaders attempted to turn the emperor into a public figure around whom they could rally popular feeling and support.

They built an ideology on his claim to direct descent from the ancestral deities of Shinto myth, translating that claim into the idiom of kinship by taking the ie as a model for the entire nation. The emperor's line thus became the senior line from which all others had branched; all Japanese therefore owed him loyalty as the head of the national household. Turning outward, the Meiji leaders also used the imperial institution in the conduct of foreign relations. In support of Japan's claim to equal status with nations of the West, the emperor was likened to European monarchs; he was even made to adopt the clothing and demeanor of his Western counterparts (Gluck 1985: 73–101; Smith 1983: 15–20).

The wedding ritual devised for the Crown Prince reflects the several emphases present in this political use of the imperial institution. As a religious ceremony it served as an analogue to the Christian weddings of European royalty. As a Shinto ceremony it was appropriate to the emperor's central place in Shinto mythology. It also served as a public statement about the changes that had come with the new order, a statement whose message was abundantly clear. An editorial in the *Asahi Shimbun* on the day of the wedding proclaimed that the elaborate ceremony was merely restoring imperial weddings to their proper place, after centuries of neglect. The Restoration, in other words, had set the world right.

Shortly after the imperial wedding, shrines began to receive requests from commoners for similar ceremonies (Bacon 1902: 435–36), and within a few years the Shinto wedding was a regular service at large shrines in major cities.[2] Ultimately, in the postwar period, as we have seen, the commercial wedding industry incorporated both the ceremony and the reception into a pattern of services that today enjoys nearly universal popularity. The basic outlines of the ceremony have changed little since its inception, although in recent decades the ring exchange has been added as a regular feature. Another change involves the wedding vows. These have long been part of the ceremony, but where they were once read by the nakōdo, who thereby swore to his responsibility for the success of the marriage, they are nowadays almost always read by the groom.

The ceremony as it has thus evolved is heterogeneous, weaving together several traditions. Some of its elements, like the ring exchange and the reading of the vows, are modern customs that have been borrowed from the West. Others, such as the *san-san-ku-do* and the nakōdo, derive from the schools of ceremonial etiquette established by the samurai before the Tokugawa period. The invocation (*norito*), purification (*harai*), and offering (of *tamagushi*), all traditional elements of Shinto worship, are older still. These elements make the ceremony decidedly Shinto, but do not make it a wedding, since they are all included in Shinto rites performed on a variety of other occasions. This is another indication of the ceremony's heterogeneous nature: it is part Shinto ceremony and part wedding ritual.

But participants may be only vaguely conscious of the meanings associated with the Shinto aspects of the ceremony. The underlying concern with purity in Shinto ritual, and accordingly the significance of the harai as an act of purification, are both well known. Less understood is the act of exchange that takes place in the rite, in which the principals who receive the blessings of the kami (deities) are returning the favor by presenting the tamagushi, symbolizing an offering of cloth. The employee who explains the ceremony's procedures to the wedding group beforehand made no mention of this aspect during the several occasions I was present as witness. Nor did he point out that the *sake* used differs from ordinary *sake*, for the kami have blessed it by partaking of it and now share it with the bridal pair. He merely stressed each time that it was a solemn ceremony. It is indeed the solemnity of the occasion that appears to be the most salient feature for the participants, and one that they uniformly approve. Even an informant who roundly criticized all other aspects of the commercialized wedding was impelled to praise it on this point. She had felt obliged to go along with whatever her husband's family wished—since he was a chōnan who was taking over the family store, and many of the guests were important business associates—but she remained inwardly detached and even resentful throughout the proceedings. Most of the wedding struck her as silly, she claims, except for the Shinto ceremony: "That at least had a certain amount of solemnity to it."

That the Shinto ceremony is understood by all as a solemn event is entirely appropriate for the task it begins of articulating society's basic values into an image of the ideal marital roles. The elements that perform this function, however, are not specific to the Shinto ceremony; they are found in contemporary Buddhist and nonreligious wedding ceremonies as well.[3] The symbolic value of one of these, the newlyweds' exchange of *sake* (*san-san-ku-do*), to the image thus produced is signaled by its alternate name of *meoto katame no sakazukigoto*—the *sake* pledge for the bonding of husband and wife. In secular ceremonies such pledges made with an exchange of *sake* have long been a means of sealing agreements that create social bonds; the similar meaning in Shinto ritual of presenting *sake* and subsequently partaking of it, as a way of creating bonds between the gods and men, has just been noted. Other *sake* exchanges that follow in the ceremony amplify on this theme: the *oyako katame* ("bonding of parents and children") *sakazukigoto* and the *shinzoku katame* ("bonding of relatives") *sakazukigoto*. The *san-san-ku-do* thus announces the bond created by the wedding between the couple in their new status of husband and wife, an interconnectedness that is made emphatic through its series of repeated exchanges.

An embellishment of the *san-san-ku-do* amplifies the theme of bonding. Each of the two vessels from which the *sake* is poured is decorated with a piece of origami representing a stylized butterfly, attached by *mizuhiki*, strings made of colored paper. It is the mizuhiki that are of interest here, for in Japan the act of tying symbolizes the formation of a social bond. Thus like our English idiom "tying the knot," the Japanese phrase *en o musubu*—"tie the (social) connection"—means to get married. Mizuhiki also figure in the giving of gifts, especially those that one family gives another on the occasion of a birth, marriage, illness, or death, or those that are given at customary times during the year to maintain social relationships. These items always bear a piece of white paper, the *noshigami*, on top of the gift's decorative wrapping, on which the giver writes his name and the occasion of the gift. Formerly mizuhiki were commonly used to tie up the entire package, the preference for mixing two different colors perhaps mirroring the gift's social function of conjoining disparate entities. Nowadays it is more common for images of the mizuhiki to be printed directly on the noshigami. Rules governing the selection of colors are maintained, however: red and gold, red and white, silver and gold, or any of these colors alone may be used with gifts for auspicious occasions; white and black or white and silver are used for those connected with funerary or memorial rites.

For auspicious events the paper will also have a special printed mark, or *noshi*—a further permutation of what began as a slice of dried abalone attached to the gift, then became a piece of origami representing the fish, and ended up as a representation of the origami substitute. Formerly the noshi was routinely attached to gifts other than those for funerary or memorial events to denote the occasion did not call for abstention from eating fish. A real origami, also called noshi when folded in this shape, is now used only on very elaborate occasions, as in the presentation of the betrothal gifts. But it would be a mistake to see the reductions involved—from an actual piece of shellfish to an origami representation to the origami's printed image, or similarly from real mizuhiki to their printed images—as indicating that the symbolic meaning of these elements has faded to the point where they have become purely decorative. For it is still the images of the noshi and the mizuhiki, or the mizuhiki alone, that differentiate noshigami from ordinary paper and announce the fact of the gift. They also indicate, by their colors and presence (or absence), the type of gift.

If the mizuhiki thus augment the *san-san-ku-do*'s announcement of the social bond created by the wedding, the presence of the nakōdo, and the couple's close association with him and his wife throughout the wedding, demonstrate the nature of this bond. I have already discussed the symbolic dimension of the nakōdo's role: usually an older man and preferably socially prominent as well, he has shown his ability to lead a stable married life and stands as a symbol of the successful union. The bridal pair's association with the nakōdo thus asserts the permanence of the marital bond imaged in the *san-san-ku-do*.

That association also points out the couple's isolation from the rest of the group—an isolation understandable in terms of the wedding's structure as a rite of passage, as the means of setting the stage for the articulation of the wedding's symbolic themes. Historically this isolation was more complete. In ethnographic accounts of prewar and early postwar home weddings, in which the ceremony consisted essentially of the *san-san-ku-do*, the exchange is described variously as taking place in a separate room;

as occurring behind a screen; and as being attended only by the nakōdo or someone to pour the *sake*.[4] In the contemporary Shinto ceremony the physical isolation is less extreme, but it is there nonetheless. Together with the nakōdo, the bride and groom sit in the center of the shrine room, apart from the rest of the group. And they maintain something of this isolation during the reception, also sitting with the nakōdo but apart from the guests. They of course talk and have contact with other people throughout the day, but their isolation from the group—in terms of having separate positions—ends only when they mingle directly with the guests at the close of the reception. This state of relative isolation serves to symbolize their departure from their old status, a symbolism that is reinforced by the wedding clothes they wear. Their costumes, like the formal outfits of all Japanese brides and grooms, bear no signs of the wearers' former social identities.

It is while the principals are in this symbolically liminal state that the marital bond they will form is announced by the *san-san-ku-do* and its permanence asserted by the nakōdo's presence. Both themes are reinforced by the wedding vows. In White Crane Palace's standard version, the bride and groom pledge "to . . . spend all the days of our lives together with unchanging trust and eternal affection." They further promise "to make our hearts as one [and] give mutual help and support," a note that the priest who conducts the ceremony echoes at the end when he instructs the newlyweds to build a harmonious home. These themes are expanded on and others articulated during the reception, beginning with the cake-cutting ceremony.

The Cake-Cutting Ceremony

The cake-cutting ceremony is a relatively recent phenomenon. Wedding cakes first drew popular attention in the early postwar period, when they became a common feature of the lavish and highly publicized weddings of celebrities, but their general acceptance did not come until much later. White Crane Palace began offering wedding cakes to its customers in 1970, but unlike the wax or rubber cakes of today, the first ones were real, and were cut and served at the reception. Real cakes were expensive, however, over $250 at today's prices, and demand was low. The introduction of artificial cakes in 1973 greatly reduced the cost, but it was not until several years later that the cake-cutting ceremony attained its present universal popularity. Although the ceremony is an optional service, recall that almost 96 percent of the customers elect it.

Why has the cake-cutting ceremony become so popular, and in such a remarkably short period of time? Surely the desire to emulate the rich and famous and the attraction toward things Western that has marked the postwar period are factors. But neither of these has any bearing on the cake's symbolic content. That the cake is inedible, moreover, demands that we look for some symbolic significance—or be forced otherwise to conclude that the custom is patently absurd.

Let me suggest that an entire nation cannot be so silly and faddish, that in fact conceptual associations already present in Japanese culture enabled the wedding cake to assume a symbolic value parallel to the one it holds in the West—as an image of fertility—though not necessarily in the same fashion. Wedding cakes have been seen in Western tradition as grain products, and like the rice thrown at the bride, are connected with images of seeds and insemination. The modern usage evidently evolved from the English custom of breaking a cookie over the bride's head, a practice tracing back to Roman society and related to the more general use of fruits, nuts, grain, and grain products in ceremonies intended to bring fertility and prosperity (Scott 1953: 238; Westermarck 1926: 193–95). Thus in the English tradition the cookie crumbs were gathered up and eaten by the guests both to ensure the bride's fertility and to bring fortune to those who consumed them.

Modern-day events may still illustrate these associations vividly. When the wedding of the heir to the British throne kept alive the tradition of having separate cakes for the bride and groom, the chefs of Her Majesty's Navy provided Prince Charles with a fruit cake—replete with nuts and raisins. As it happens, the Japanese have a similar tradition of taking seeds and grain as metaphors for human fertility. When a samurai bride entered the palanquin that would take her to the groom's home, grains of rice were sprinkled inside, along with other fertility symbols.[5] In modern speech *tane* ("seed") is used as a colloquial term for semen; and a woman may be called *hatake*, a "field."

But the link between fertility and the wedding cake in Japan may derive from two different associations. One has to do with the distinction drawn between sweet-tasting things (*amai*) and those that are spicy or pungent (*karai*). The Japanese apply this opposition broadly, using it to distinguish salty from bland dishes, as well as hot from sweet ones. They also use it to divide up the social world, through the association of certain classes of people with certain types of foods. Men, who are generally expected to be fond of drinking, are said to prefer the karai or drier brands of *sake*; women, who are not expected to like *sake* much, are said to drink only the sweeter varieties. Alcohol in general is classed as one of the spicy foods, which are the province of adults, and which children are taught to avoid in favor of amai foods. "*Karai yo!*" ("It's spicy!") is the standard phrase parents use to steer toddlers away from foods that they do not want them to have, for whatever reason. Sometimes it is because such things really are karai, like curries made with a lot of spices. Curry made especially for children, by contrast, contains more sweet ingredients like fruit and is called amai.

The cake may therefore symbolize fertility in the wedding through its sweetness, rather than as a grain product, by drawing on this broader association of sweets with children—which the marriage is meant to produce. The same association may account for the prominence of the Western-style cakes now featured not only at children's birthday parties but also at Christmas. Indeed Christmas is even more clearly an affair for children in this non-Christian nation than in the West: children receive presents from their parents, but make no gift in return, and the counterpart of our family gathering centers not on dinner, but rather—and again primarily for the benefit of the children—on a decorated white "Christmas cake." One longtime Japanese friend dreads the coming of Christmas for precisely this reason, since his three children insist that he join them in sharing the cake. Like most true *sake* lovers, he prefers the foods classed with *sake* as *karai* and professes to dislike sweets.

In any event, the association of cakes with children predates such Western influences as Christmas or the wedding cake. Embree (1939: 180) reports that at the naming ceremony of a newborn child in Suye "a tray of formal congratulatory cake is served. The cake . . . is made of dry rice flour pressed into shapes of *tai* fish, pine, plum, and bushy-tailed tortoise, the traditional Japanese symbols of good fortune and long life, and into the shape of Momotarō coming out of a peach." The reference to the popular folktale of Momotarō points to the other association that may link the wedding cake to fertility in the mind of the Japanese. Not only is the peach "a female sex symbol in Japan," as Embree notes, but there is a symbolic rendering of the sexual act in the story itself. It opens with a childless old couple; the woman, while washing clothes in the river, finds an enormous peach and brings it home. When her husband cuts it open—with a large kitchen knife—out pops a little boy, whose adventures occupy the rest of the tale.

One can hardly ignore the phallic symbolism of the knife in the cake-cutting ceremony, or the reading of its insertion, the central act of the ceremony on which all proceedings fixate, as a metaphor for coitus. Moreover, the act is highly marked linguistically. Because of the prohibition on the word "cut" at weddings, inauspiciously suggesting a phrase ("cut the connection") used to describe the dissolution of social bonds, the emcee introduces the cake-cutting with the stilted and suggestive circumlocution *nyūtō*—literally, "the insertion of the sword." Of course sexual interpretations are not always consciously present in the minds of those who observe the ceremony, or of those who hear the folktale, for that matter. But the connection suggests itself readily enough. It was first pointed out to me by a friend, a shopkeeper blessed with the townsman's traditionally earthy sense of humor, at a wedding we attended in the mid-1970s. When the emcee announced the "insertion of the sword," my friend suddenly nudged my arm. "Oh, *nyūtō*, *nyūtō*!" he whispered, with an impish grin, and with both hands at his crotch, fist on fist, he waggled his hips in the appropriate motion.

The possibility of a purely Japanese gloss on the cake-cutting ceremony helps make its recent and rapid acceptance far more understandable. For by drawing on associations already articulated in Japanese culture—the association of cakes with children and the act of cutting with coitus—the ceremony now appropriately supplements the ideal image of the husband/wife relationship set out by the *san-san-ku-do* and the presence of the nakōdo. Marriage, according to this ideal, is a close bond between husband and wife that is expected to last. Equally important, it is expected to produce children. This interpretation, moreover, gives us a way of dealing with the fact that the cake is inedible: if its function is to *symbolize* reproduction and children, it may then, as a symbolic element, be subject to the same process of abstraction that has reduced the noshi from a real piece of shellfish to the printed image of a piece of folded paper—without losing its ability to signify.

Furthermore, we may see the cake-cutting ceremony as taking over this function from a symbolic element whose ability to invoke the same associations appears to be waning. Recall that the vessels used in the *san-san-ku-do* are decorated with origami butterflies, one male and the other female. While these are sometimes interpreted as referring to marital constancy, after the butterflies' habit of flirting about in pairs (Casal 1940: 121), their manipulation during the ceremony in the Tokugawa period points to another interpretation: first the *mechō*, the female butterfly, was removed from one vessel and set down in an upward facing position, then the *ochō* (male butterfly) was removed and laid "face down on top of the *mechō*" (Ema 1971: 151). If this too may be read as imaging the (human) sexual act, it is not surprising that in later times the ceremonial *sake* was often poured by children, usually a young girl and boy, who were called the ochō and mechō. In Hirayama this practice survived in urban weddings until the commercialized wedding completely supplanted ceremonies held at home; several informants recall observing it around 1960. In rural areas the custom was still followed in the mid-1970s.[6] But with the current universal popularity of the Shinto wedding, in which the *sake* is poured by shrine maidens, this dimension of the ceremony has undoubtedly become obscure.

The wedding industry has chosen to use the cake-cutting to emphasize other social values as well. As noted in Chapter 1, in the script that White Crane Palace provides to emcees, the cake-cutting is introduced as "the first step of cooperation in the couple's new life," echoing a note sounded in the wedding vows. Emcees who choose to write their own scripts may similarly announce it as a demonstration of marital harmony. The theme of harmony is further expressed not only in the narration accompanying the cutting, but also in the care given to let everyone who wishes to do so to photograph the couple as they cut the cake.

The wedding hall's carefully engineered image of cooperation and harmony is further articulated in the speeches made by the nakōdo and the guests. The need for cooperation between husband and wife, for mutual support and understanding, is one of the commonest themes, particularly in the speeches of the nakōdo and shuhin, who are likely to set out moral precepts for the couple to follow in their life ahead. "Please work hard together to build a good home" is the formula most frequently heard, but many speakers find different words to express the same idea. One nakōdo declared his hope that "by giving each other mutual help and encouragement, going forward a step at a time, the couple will build a healthy and happy home." A shuhin stated that "for married couples the feeling of being a team together is always necessary. . . . I hope you never forget that feeling and will build a home full of compassion." In pointing out the agreement between the speeches and the cake-cutting ceremony in portraying marriage as a harmonious relationship, let me emphasize again that such images are stereotypes never fully realized in everyday life. Nevertheless, the agreement testifies to the power of this image for the Japanese. It is one that they feel ought to be set out for brides and grooms as they prepare to become husband and wives: the ideal of a close and lasting marital bond, harmonious, cooperative, and blessed with children.

But this image hardly suggests a profound difference between Japan and other societies, for what people do not celebrate marriage in similar terms? It is only when we look more closely at the image, and at others produced by the wedding—only when we plot them against the larger backdrop of values they encode—that differences emerge, differences concerning the most basic concepts of gender, person, and society itself. In the next chapter I continue my analysis of the wedding's symbolic content as it illuminates these concepts.

SIX

Gender, Person, and Society

The image of marital harmony portrayed in the wedding industry's elaborate cake-cutting ceremony and echoed in the guests' speeches does not embody the ideal of sexual equality. Far from it: in the wedding hall's narrative script the bride happily declares her willingness to follow the groom's silent lead; the bride who wrote her own narration (Chap. 1) celebrates her happiness at having found someone on whom she can be dependent. Wedding speakers frequently remind brides of their duty to devote themselves to their husbands, injunctions often translated into ideal images of the division of labor: men are charged with the important task of going out in the world to work, women with the subordinate role of supporting their husbands by running the home. One groom's boss declared: "I ask the bride to give her fullest support to the groom, so that he can do his best work." The boss of another groom told the bride: "When men go out to work in the world, things don't always go their way. When they come home, they wish to have everything their way, so please obey whatever your husband says as though you were a child."

There are instances, of course, when a speaker will recognize that the situation calls for a different tack. Noting that the bride would continue to work after marriage, one person advised: "Since both of you may come home tired from work, you cannot live by the old adage that a man has no place in the kitchen, but must be more flexible." But the majority hold to more rigid stereotypes. One bride's former employer told her that "providing good and delicious food for your husband is your first job as a wife." The fact that most of the speakers are men, and usually older ones, may be of considerable significance, but even when younger women get a chance to speak, they rarely say anything different. The friend of one bride stated her hope that "having found such a wonderful husband, the bride will devote herself totally to him from now on"; another expressed her confidence that the bride would make a good, "charming" wife; another, in the same vein, stated that she was sure the bride would do a good job of running the home.

We may try to be as understanding of such statements as Japanologists like Smith (1987: 4), who notes how thoroughly Japanese forms of speech and styles of social interaction assume "the superiority of the male and the subordinate status of the female," and how these pervasive markers of gender inequality "provide the ground upon which the behavior and attitudes of men and women toward one another ultimately are based." But the persistence of gender inequality in Japan remains an ugly fact to Western eyes nonetheless, one whose effect on people's lives cannot be ignored. This applies to our own experiences there as well, for surely it was easier for me to live in that society than it is for American women. As a male anthropologist, moreover, I avoided many of the problems that confront my female counterparts. One colleague paints vividly the conflict she felt between her identity "as an American career woman" and the role she filled as a host family's surrogate daughter:

Most of this [conflict] centered around the issue of serving men: cooking for them, serving them before you yourself begin to eat, etc. On the occasions when the wife of the family was away for the evening, busy with one or another of her volunteer activities, it was my responsibility to cook for the husband, who would not dream of entering the kitchen when there was a woman in the house. . . . I was able to carry out my duties well, but this in turn created enormous inner conflict, because as an American woman, I disliked the very role I was obliged to play (Kondo 1982: 75–76).

Yet the gender distinctions can be fully as problematical for the male anthropologist set on presenting Japan to members of his own culture. To raise the banner of cultural relativism in matters of gender is to risk condemnation as a chauvinist; to criticize another society—by whose values?—for the way it treats women is no less questionable for its enthnocentrism. This is a true dilemma, with no solution.

We are nevertheless obliged to explain Japanese attitudes toward gender as best we can. This requires that we examine how these attitudes interrelate with other conceptual domains, not simply because gender has important links with "a wide variety of . . . institutions, relationships, ideologies, or forms of behavior" Bestor (1985: 284). For if we can see such attitudes as part of a larger whole of concepts—which individually may be no less challenging to our own ideals—we may come to appreciate a certain logical consistency in the Japanese views of gender, person, and society, a consistency that makes these views appear to the Japanese as natural and necessary, as representing the morally proper order of things.

Notions of Gender: Public vs. Domestic

Put simply, I shall argue (1) that the Japanese view gender as constituting a complementary distribution of both competence and incompetence in the activities proper to the public and domestic domains; (2) that the differing *incompetencies* thus ascribed to both men and women accord with a view of the person as incomplete, in the sense of being unable to function fully in society on his or her own; (3) that society accordingly takes as its basic unit not the individual but relational wholes, and demands that individuals be embedded in the most basic of these—the husband/wife unit—for valid participation in social life; and (4) that the wider realm of social relations is founded, like the husband/wife unit, on the principle of interdependence, further rendering the individual incomplete as a social being. Of the four elements in my formulation, the characterization "incomplete" most directly challenges our own notion of the person and is thus most likely to be misunderstood by the Western reader. I will address this issue in due course. First I examine a terminological division in discussions of gender that is wholly familiar: the public domain and the domestic domain. What the Japanese mean when they use these terms often appears very close to the meanings we attach to them—so much so that the subtle but telling differences are easily overlooked.

The Japanese term *katei*, for example, much like the everyday meaning of its English counterpart, domestic, conflates residence, family group, and such activities as food preparation and child rearing. Also like domestic, *katei* is a strongly spatialized concept. The word itself is written as a compound of the characters for "house" and "garden," and is glossed in Japanese dictionaries as "the place of family livelihood." As this definition suggests, the primary meaning of katei encompasses the notion of domicile, but its association with activities central to family living is clear from the content of *kateika* (literally, "katei studies")—home economics courses. Although formerly devoted largely to cooking and sewing, nowadays the curriculum has expanded to include budget management and child care.[1] A similar range of topics can be found in newspaper articles in the section commonly referred to as *kateiran* ("katei column"). Another notable focus of these articles is interfamily relations—between parents and children, husband and wife, and married children and parents who co-reside. Thus the family group— meaning primarily the nuclear but including the stem family—is also subsumed under katei.

The contrasting notion of public is conveyed by the word for society, *shakai*. Just as the word public in its ordinary English meaning is more amorphous than "domestic," so the semantic range of shakai encompasses both the world of work and the broader realm of extra-familial social relations.[2] Rohlen (1974: 49–50) has found both meanings involved in an intriguing appropriation of the term in the corporate ideology of a modern bank. At an official ceremony for new employees, the bank president reminded them that by entering the world of work they had become *shakaijin* (adult members of society). As such it was their duty to serve society and contribute to the general welfare, thereby repaying what they owed society and their parents for raising them to adulthood. By explicitly linking entrance into the bank with membership in adult society, Rohlen notes, "the implication is clearly made that fulfilling one's role [at work] serves to fulfill one's obligations to society at large."

Wedding speakers similarly use shakai and shakaijin to assert a change in the status of the bride and groom. Because of their marriage, the speakers will say, the couple now enter society anew or have finally become full members of society. Such statements often preface injunctions to the couple to conduct themselves in a socially responsible manner—admonitions that again demonstrate the semantic range of shakai, since they cover not only a person's relations at work, but his or her relations with relatives, family, and friends as well. They also make explicit the conceptual link between shakai and katei. "You will be faced with difficulties both at home [katei] and in society," one couple was warned by the groom's uncle. In another speaker's more positive formulation, the couple were urged to "build a good home [katei], and be both good husband and wife at home and exemplary citizens [*rippa na shakaijin*] outside."

The words this last speaker used for "at home" and "outside" were, respectively, <u>uchi</u> (which more generally can mean "inside" as well as "house" or "household") and *soto*, an opposition that finds widespread application in everyday life. Indeed, that opposition can be used to convey the distinction between public and domestic, but the terms are not restricted to this usage and so do not parallel public and domestic as closely as the terms shakai and katei do. Uchi is more easily abstracted from the home as a place than katei, for example, as shown by its use to distinguish one's own company, workplace, or school from other such organizations. As a result, uchi and soto do not so explicitly mark the strong genderization of the domestic domain as female, and of the public domain as male.[3]

In the wedding, which takes place in the public domain, this genderization is clearly indicated by the separate behaviors of men and women. Men are more active and do most of the public speaking, in keeping with the more general role of husbands and fathers as family representatives in such public contexts as meetings of local organizations or funerals. The bride herself exemplifies the more passive role of women in the public domain. To begin with, she is frequently obscured from or out of public view. Her bridal headdress, for example, traces back to the time when women customarily covered their heads whenever they ventured outside the home (Ema 1971: 80). Two styles of headdress have been retained; one covers the upper part of her forehead and most of her heavy wig; the other envelops the entire wig and extends down to cover some of the face.[4] In addition, the heavy white makeup, also part of the traditional bridal wear, so thoroughly masks the bride's face as to obscure her features. Both the heavy makeup and the headdress are discarded with the first ironaoshi, when the bride changes into other clothes, so that her face and expressions are clearly visible. But the ironaoshi itself forces her to be absent from much of the reception—if she has two ironaoshi, she will miss more than a third of the reception.

Although the groom also leaves for an ironaoshi, he does so only once and his change is quick; he is thus present for most of the reception, often sitting next to a vacant seat, waiting for his bride to reappear. Moreover, he is much more active than the bride even when she is by his side. He is often engaged in conversation with friends, relatives, and company associates who have come to pour him some beer or *sake* and needle him about the tension he has endured through the day, or the activity that awaits him that night. The bride's friends also come to congratulate and talk with her, but their voices and even their laughter tend to be hushed. The bride does little of the talking, moreover, and in marked contrast to the groom, she does not drink much and eats virtually nothing at all. For the most part she remains quite still, looking demurely downward or perhaps fixing her gaze on a speaker or an entertainer. In fact, apart from the times when she must get up to go and change her clothes, she normally shows little animation except when she does something like the cake-cutting together with the groom.

The duties of the nakōdo also conform to the image of the male as the publicly active member of the husband/wife unit. Even though it is as a married couple that the nakōdo and his wife serve as role models for the bride and groom, and the emcee is careful to introduce them as "Mr. and Mrs. . . ." at the time of the nakōdo's speech, it is invariably the husband who speaks. Similarly, the thank-you speech on behalf of the couple's parents at the end of the reception is always delivered by a man, usually the groom's father.[5] This is followed moments later by the newlyweds' expression of gratitude to their guests, but again it is only the groom who speaks.

If the public domain is thus marked as properly male, and the domestic by implication as female, it is important to note that the genderization applies more narrowly to shakai and katei as spatial entities. The domicile in contemporary urban life has become "very much female-oriented" the Japanese anthropologist Kurita concludes, based on his survey showing that household possessions are strongly associated with the housewife. He speculates that this is because men, removed from the home by their involvement with their companies, "have acquiesced in the organization of the home along the lines of the female principle." The visible result is modern apartments furnished with objects bearing "the color pink and floral patterns" that "reflect what women find charming or pretty," while the "only places in the home that could possibly be called male preserves are the bookshelf and liquor cabinet" (Kurita 1978: 114). In a corresponding but more limited way, the world outside the home is male-dominated space. Permanent positions in companies are almost exclusively held by men; most women have access only to jobs that are less secure and lower paying. Women who do manage to pursue professional careers, moreover, shy away from the businessman's role in which camaraderie stemming from strongly male activities (drinking, mahjong, golf) plays a large part, often selecting instead jobs in teaching, research, and government, which are less definitely marked as male (Osako 1978).[6] Similarly, there are physical areas of the world outside the home given over to the male entertainments just mentioned, and though shopping areas, for example, are distinctly feminine, women's excursions there may be seen primarily as an extension of their homemaking role.

Gender as Complementary Incompetence

More significant than the genderization of spatial realms is the association of men and women with the activities deemed appropriate for the domains of shakai and katei. As already noted, it is men who go out in the world and work, while women run the home. What is particularly telling, however, is the complementary distribution of both competence and incompetence between men and women in these activities. If men are competent at earning money by working in the public domain, then by implication women are incompetent in this respect, at least in the stereotypic view of things. This image is indeed based on a partial truth, since women are generally less likely than men to find secure and high-paying jobs. Similarly, if men are the proper representatives for the family at public functions such as meetings of local organizations and funerals, then women may discharge this role only by default, when husbands or fathers are unable to attend.

On the other hand, if money earning is an activity proper to the public domain and therefore in the competency of men, money-managing is an aspect of home care (recall that budgeting is included in the curriculum of home economics courses) and is thus in the competency of women. Men are considered less capable in this regard. They are more apt, it is said, to spend money on nonessentials such as their hobbies or leisure activities, and less likely to stick to budgets based on long-range plans, such as for the purchase of a house. In short, in the stereotypic view of things men are irresponsible; they cannot defer their gratifications. This image too is based on at least a partial truth. Men engage more in socializing at bars and restaurants, where they are apt to overspend for fear of appearing stingy. On the average they manage to save less money before marriage than women, even though they have worked for just as long or longer, and at higher salaries.[7] After marriage it is the wife who is seen as keeping the family budget within reasonable bounds, and in the stereotypic domestic arrangement, the husband hands his monthly pay envelope over to his wife, who in turn hands him back his pocket money.

The notion of male irresponsibility extends to other duties also ascribed to the domestic domain. Men are unable to live by themselves, it is often said, or if they do, they will not live properly—they will not keep things neat, they will not eat regularly, and so forth. Here too the stereotype bears an element of truth. While I was conducting my research, the media reported the results of a survey showing that two-thirds of male college students, who generally live alone in single-room apartments, go off to class in the morning without breakfast. This prompted comment among the group with which I worked most closely at White Crane Palace, the directors and two women who oversee the tasks of getting the food and drinks in the ballrooms on schedule. Both women are middle-aged and married. Though they work at least as hard as the directors, at coffee breaks and meals it is always they who do the preparing, serving, and cleaning up. At one such break talk touched on the recent survey, and the general difficulty that single men have caring for themselves. Drawing on past experience, one of the directors declared: "Making something to eat is too much trouble. It's so much simpler to open a bottle of beer and a bag of crackers. Maybe it's easier these days with instant noodles and whatever, but if men live by themselves they just don't eat regularly." After the conversation the men left their coffee cups in the sink for the women to wash. All of this went on, I should add, in an organization that employs professional male cooks and professional male dishwashers. Apparently the performance of these activities as work in the public domain poses no threat to the deeply held view of male incompetence at home.

A similar experience years earlier underscores the point that competence in one domain fails to translate into competence in the other. Among a party at a restaurant were a young woman who was studying for a career as a music teacher and her mother. At one point I caught the two absorbed in watching a chef painstakingly preparing an omelette for use in sushi. The omelette is made by repeatedly pouring thin layers of batter into a small skillet, each one becoming a new outer coating for the carefully folded mass of cooked egg. After several minutes one of the women remarked: "Wouldn't you know it. It has to be a man's job." The import was that without the chef's intense concentration on his task—a male trait appropriate to the domain of work—one could not perform the job; a woman's domestic cooking skills would simply not suffice.

I suggest that the strength of such views stems from a belief that a broad range of male and female differences—including the complementary abilities and inabilities in the domains of shakai and katei—is ultimately grounded in nature. Japanese parents readily express the opinion that baby boys are innately more active and boisterous than girls. Further, more than 60 percent of the respondents in a recent survey said they believed also in "inborn differences between males and females in their ability to think about and settle issues" (Prime Minister's Statistical Office 1980: 579). Nor do parents wish to pit nurture against nature; other surveys show even greater majorities agreeing that "it's best to raise boys in a masculine [*otokorashii*] and girls in a feminine [*onnarashii*] manner" (pp. 122, 273). The facts of nature are to be cultivated, not remade.

If I have emphasized the incompetencies, or the negative side of the differential abilities thus ascribed to men and women as natural facts, it is because I believe the view of gender as a sharing of incompetence across the domains of shakai and katei is of help in understanding, first of all, the high value the Japanese assign marriage. As mentioned in Chapter 3, the imperative to marry explains the continuing significance of the miai as an efficient strategy for finding prospective marriage partners. There are other indicators of the strength of this imperative, and the importance of marriage that it signals. Very few Japanese men remain single: less than 3 percent of those aged 45–49 have never married, against 12 percent in England and 15 percent in Sweden (United Nations 1977). As we have seen, the amount of money spent on getting married is also high—averaging $25,000 in 1981–82 (Table 2), almost twice the yearly income of the typical groom. And while marital relations may not be as cooperative and harmonious as wedding speakers urge the couple to make them, the Japanese divorce rate is only one-quarter that of the United States (United Nations 1983). In short marriage in Japan is nearly universal, is celebrated in a big way, and is expected to last.

Japanese notions of gender make marriage necessary because individuals—both men and women—are always incomplete; their deficiencies, moreover, are complementary. Men need women to manage both their money and their domestic lives. Women need men to provide economic security and proper representation for the family in the public domain. Marriage thus cannot be thought of merely as an event that, if it chances to happen at the right time and in the right way, makes some individuals happier than others. It is necessary for the very practical reason that men and women happen to be competent where their opposites are not, incapable of doing what the other does well, and both in need of each other to get along.

The Shape of Social Participation

The notion of gender as a complementarity of incompetence has a larger significance, since its view of individuals as incomplete on the practical plane extends to the moral plane as well. For individuals are equally incomplete as persons—as social actors performing their roles.

To begin with, a person is always regarded at some level as belonging to larger relational wholes, social groups defined as

sets of interconnected roles. The most fundamental of these is
the katei, in its sense of the family. All individuals belong to a
katei—either the one of their birth or the one they form at marriage. But it is only when they establish their own katei that
people are seen as fully achieving the status of shakaijin, as
wedding speakers frequently note. "The bride and groom are
taking their first step today as members of society [shakaijin],"
declared the uncle of a groom. "Until now no one recognized
them as such, but as of today everyone should treat them as
fully adult [*ichininmae no ningen*]." The term *ichininmae* ("adult")
can also imply independence, for in establishing their own katei
the principals are no longer junior members in their parents' katei. This was clearly the intent of the speaker who appropriated
the meaning of katei as physical residence to talk about the family as a social unit: "Since the bride and groom have just completed building a new home for their marital residence, they will
henceforth be, in both name and substance, independent members of society." But though they may have been thus character-
ized as independent (*dokuritsu*), the term carried no claim of
their independence of the wider society, a point to which I shall
presently return.

Such statements clarify the conceptual link between katei and
shakai, since forming the one is prerequisite to participating in
the other. Here is another reason why the Japanese are so serious about getting married, for the failure to do so carries the
severe implications of immaturity and lack of moral responsibility. One male informant who married late recalls that, when he
reached the age of thirty, his boss began to tell him how continued bachelorhood would cause increasing problems with
both fellow workers and business associates from other companies—how they would begin to wonder why he continued to
avoid taking on the responsibilities of married life, would begin
to have doubts about how deeply he could be trusted and about
his ability to serve as a representative of his company. For the
same reasons the injunction made by wedding speakers to the
bride and groom to work harmoniously and build a good home
is a heavy one, and accordingly the newlyweds respond at the
end of the wedding with their pledge to "work hard together"
and "give our best efforts in beginning our new life" by "building a bright and happy home [*akarui katei*]."

The speech containing this pledge is of course made by the groom, acting in his role as the couple's proper representative in the public domain. This raises the point that as a social group katei is not genderized. It cannot be, for even if its other components of domicile and activity are regarded as exclusively or largely female, katei as a social unit is formed only through the conjunction of male and female as husband and wife. The concepts of shakai and katei, together with the notion of gender as a complementarity of incompetence, thus help maintain a view of society that stands in sharp contrast to our own moral universe by not privileging the autonomy of the individual. For the Japanese individuals fully participate in society only through their roles as core members of their family group, only by maintaining their own katei. In actuality this requires a combination of activities at which men and women are seen as competent and incompetent in complementary fashion. The solution—marriage—is at once practical and moral, the socially proper response to facts naturally given.

The Individual and Society

The moral argument that the person is incomplete requires more of individuals than maintaining their own home. It extends outside the katei as well, for here too individuals are held to be incapable of getting along by themselves.

Before pursuing this point further, let us pause briefly to note where that argument seems to be implicitly heading. It requires but a short logical step to go from the assertion of such a moral view—by which the individual must always rely on others and can act only as an embedded member of relational wholes—to the conclusion that this view promotes collectivistic and group-oriented social interaction. It is a step beset by pitfalls, however. For if the image of the Japanese as group-oriented resembles all stereotypes in "contain[ing] some elements of truth," it may also amount, "however unintentionally, . . . to an ethnic snub," warns Plath (1980: 4): "The person who is 'dependent,' whose self is 'submerged,' who has 'weak and permeable ego boundaries'—phrases applied to the Japanese—is by Western measures immature. He can scarcely be acknowledged to be 'his own man.'" The same can be said of the phrase "incomplete."

It is necessary, in short, to add depth to the stereotype of the Japanese as "collectivistic" as opposed to our own "individualism" in order to capture some of "the tempo and tenor of ordinary lives." Yet it is ill-advised to ignore the stereotype altogether, or worse, claim it must be wrong.[8] To do so fails to take full account of the process by which such images are given a particular positive or negative tone. If contrasting the Japanese as group oriented and Westerners as individualistic can be read as a snub to Japan in terms of our values, then that contrast can also be read as a snub to the West in terms of the Japanese notions of the individual and society. This is precisely what happened every time Tomiko told me "Americans are selfish." For anyone who asserts he is his own man, complete in himself, is by definition *wagamama*—selfish, heedless of his interdependence with others, unwilling to recognize and accede to the constraints that social relations invariably entail. In short, like the child who thinks only of himself, he is immature.

Of course the danger exists that, in focusing on what a society says is the way things ought to be, we will lose sight of the differences between the image and the reality. No matter how much the Japanese may assert, at ritual moments like the wedding or at company entrance ceremonies, that people should devote themselves wholeheartedly to certain morally proper roles, what society so thoroughly socializes its members that they follow its norms unthinkingly? As individuals the Japanese are indeed aware of the selves that stand apart from their social roles and give continuity to the "portfolio of identities" they hold in the larger society. At times they may agree to fill these roles only with great reluctance. Or they may not agree at all, and thus strain the limits of variability in preferred pathways that society offers.[9]

The overwhelming consensus in analyses of Japan holds nevertheless that it *is* a more group-oriented society than most, in both its behavior and its ideals, despite the conflicts that individuals must always experience with their roles as persons. Surely, as Smith (1983: 98) claims, this attests to a definition of maturity as precisely the ability to constrain one's selfish desires and submit to the demands that social participation entails. The Japanese, he goes on to note, are fully aware of the difficulties involved:

A recurrent theme in novels, plays, and film is the exploration of the ways in which the young and the strong-willed attempt to resolve the conflicts that arise in the process of coming to terms with the demands of society. Those who fail to do so, whether because they will not or cannot, are the tragic heroes and heroines of fiction and the press. . . . For ordinary mortals, however, there are in daily use many words that reflect recognition of the need to accommodate, to endure, to bear, to accept, and to relinquish—*gaman, shimbō, akirame* among them. All are words in daily use to children, kin, friends, and colleagues whom one is urging to come to terms—and thereby demonstrate neither submissiveness nor passivity, but true maturity.

That maturity, moreover, means nothing less than admitting one's incompleteness as a person. Let me caution against misinterpretation once again, for the image I am presenting stands in direct opposition to the Western moral ideal of autonomy. But in Japan the mature individual is fully enmeshed in the tangle of social obligation and knows it. "The meaning of being an adult," observes Kondo (1982: 61), "is to realize one's connectedness to others and to learn how to maintain those links."

We need look no farther than the wedding for an image of this maturity—and for a road map to the principals' future as adult members of society. They are found in the candle service and flower presentation, the second and third major events of the reception. Both resemble the cake-cutting ceremony in featuring ideal images of social relations, images elaborately constructed by the commercial specialists. Both are also, like the cake-cutting, recent additions to the wedding, and thus provide clues to the reasons for the wedding industry's success, a subject I shall return to in the final chapter.

The Candle Service

The candle service further resembles the cake-cutting ceremony in dramatizing the husband/wife relationship created by the wedding. But the locus of dramatic emphasis shifts: whereas the cake-cutting portrays the content of the relationship—as consisting ideally of harmonious cooperation and as producing children—the candle service shows the relationship's external aspects, by encapsulating the entire process through which it comes into being and endures in the larger society.

The central element of the service is of course the flame. This is used first to symbolize the manner in which the new social unit is formed from existing ones: just as the bride and groom are seen as members of their own families until their marriage, the flame with which they light their own candle is that of their parents.[10] The flame is also used to image the ideal of an enduring relationship. The newlyweds' candle is marked from top to bottom with a series of lines, numbered from one to twenty-five. Alerted to this fact by the director, the emcee frequently includes in his narration an invitation to the couple to burn the candle down to the appropriate line on each of their first twenty-five anniversaries. He is also likely to make the theme of endurance explicit. The script provided by White Crane Palace suggests that he ask the guests to applaud as the two of them light the candle, "so that this flame of love will burn forever in the couple's hearts." The emcee quoted in Chapter 1, in a narration he supplied himself, similarly asked the couple to "nurture this flame to make it endure and burn brightly."

Finally, the flame serves to illustrate how the new unit's enduring existence in society is ideally to be achieved. During the service the bride and groom always move together to spread their flame to each table of friends, relatives, and company associates, groups with whom they will henceforth interact as the single unit of husband and wife. As they light the candles on the tables, the emcee acknowledges the couple's debt to each group for its support in the past and proclaims their need for its continuing guidance in the future: "Thanks to all the bride's relatives. Please continue to give your support and encouragement. . . . Thanks to the friends of the couple. Please watch over them with continued benevolence." The candle service thus acts out values that contrast sharply with Western individualistic ideals. It shows society as made up of groups, not individuals. It accordingly denies the principals individual autonomy, since it portrays them as having social identities only as part of the family units in which they are always embedded, as either children or married adults. It stresses, moreover, that as an adult one cannot get along in the world without the support of superiors, relatives, family, and friends, that the individual is engaged in networks of social relations that make him or her an interdependent, rather than an independent, member of society.

This projection of the couple's future relations with the guests is reiterated in the speeches of the groom and his father (or the surrogate) at the end of the reception. Here too, at precisely the moment when the bride and groom are said to enter society as full adults, their continuing dependence on those they have invited to the wedding for guidance and support is declared. These speeches, moreover, open with firm denials of the couple's maturity, despite their married status. "The couple is still immature," asserts the groom's father, a point the groom himself echoes a few minutes later. "We are as yet a selfish and inexperienced couple," one groom declared; "we are not really fully mature adults," said another. Such statements are almost always preludes to requests for future assistance from the guests. One groom frankly admitted to anxieties about his own abilities in framing his request: "Since we are still quite immature, I fear that in the future we will be a source of trouble for everyone, so I beg you to give us your guidance." The elder brother of another groom, speaking in place of their deceased father, put the matter in more positive terms: "Although they are still immature, with the help of your encouragement, advice, and guidance, I believe they will increasingly be able to prove admirable citizens in the future. Therefore I beg your continued support."

Whereas to Westerners the notions of maturity, adulthood, and self-reliance are all bound together as natural consequences of the assertion of individual autonomy, for the Japanese the three are clearly separate. Their moral universe, moreover, is driven not by the assertion of autonomy, but rather by the notion of incompleteness. As male and female, individuals are incomplete in their competencies and thus compelled to marry. Only then are they considered fully adult. But this hardly means that they may then make the claim of self-reliance, even as a married couple. Rather, they face the continual need to rely on others with whom they will interact throughout their adult lives. Finally, maturity does not come automatically with adulthood, but is achieved only through full recognition and acceptance of the inevitable consequences of one's incompleteness, of one's interrelatedness with others.

The need to come to terms with one's incompleteness as a person is further stressed by a view of society as diffcult and unforgiving, a view complementing the belief that the individual cannot go it alone. "Together you must sail forth into society's rough waves," as one groom's uncle put it in his congratulatory speech, adding, "there will be times when the going is difficult." It is a pervasive theme: "There will no doubt be many rough times ahead for these two in society," advised a nakōdo; and the uncle of another groom admonished: "From here on you can only expect the world to be strict and demanding." Many speakers caution that with their new status "the couple's responsibilities in society will become much greater," but for the Japanese such responsibilities are not a challenge for individuals to meet on their own. "None of us can survive by ourselves alone; we all live by the grace of others," declared a bride's uncle. In a society of rough waves, no man is an island.

The Flower Presentation

The couple's passage to adulthood is further commented on by the third main event of the reception, the flower presentation. This resembles the cake-cutting and the candle service in the commercial specialists' care to accentuate its central image with lights, background music, and narration. But it differs strikingly in its focus. The emphasis shifts from the husband/ wife relationship to the bond between the principals and their parents. The flower presentation thus paradoxically provides an image not of the social relationship coming into being, but of the one that in a sense is coming to an end. To be sure, the biological and emotional ties between parents and children are not erased by marriage. But the social definition of the newlyweds as dependents, as children in the sense of having no independent identities, dissolves with their entrance into society as full members who have formed their own social unit.[11]

Of the several possible ways to approach this paradox, the simplest is to read this image as also a projection of the principals' future as adults, using imagery conveniently at hand. For the message of the cake-cutting ceremony that the marriage is supposed to produce children is echoed in the narration often used in the flower presentation: "We too are soon to become mother and father ourselves."[12] In this regard the ceremony's idealization of the roles involved—which it portrays as selfless parental sacrifice and proper filial gratitude—is appropriate in

the same way as the principals' roles as husband and wife are ⎫
idealized as harmonious and cooperative.   ⎰

Still, this hardly explains the amount of sheer emotional power
the ceremony generates. A better way to account for this emotional impact, and hence another explanation for the ceremony
itself, is found in a similar kind of retrospective idealization: the
process that takes place in ancestor worship, which in Japan involves the periodic remembrance of departed family members.
Memories of a person, however vivid immediately after his or
her death, gradually fade with time, a process that is reflected in
the series of memorial rites marking the soul's gradual progress
to purer stages of existence in the afterlife. Smith (1974) points
out that the content of worship is in many respects a continuation of the relationship the living had with a particular individual in his lifetime. But the character of the relationship is altered
by blocking out or glossing over some of its particularities. This
process, I suggest, shows that the bad in ancestors is more easily
forgotten than the good. Thus a common practice focuses on,
and helps preserve the memory of, one of the more agreeable of
individual differences: the offering at the family altar of the
kinds of food the deceased particularly enjoyed in life. "Even
where the relationship between the deceased and the survivor
was very bad, the practices of offering favorite foods—and
more—may be observed" (Smith 1974: 134). As a result the less
congenial characteristics of the person fade more quickly from
memory.

During my earlier stay in Japan I observed this process first-
hand, when Shimazaki Keisuke, my grandmother's younger
brother, died at the age of seventy-six from emphysema. The
Shimazakis' prosperity had been gained largely through the industry of this man, who for close to fifty years had worked
nearly every day in the family store. But for the last ten years of
his life his illness rendered him feeble and dependent. He spent
most of his time in the back part of the house, huddled over the
kerosene stove on winter days, listening to a transistor radio, his
eyes too weak either to read a newspaper or to watch television for very long. Most of his interactions with other family
members took the form of nagging requests for something he
wanted or felt they should do. When the time came for his

granddaughter, the eldest child, to enter high school, his anxiety to have the matter settled quickly forced an early decision to enroll her in a private school of poor academic quality where she was certain of acceptance.[13] Although the family is secure in its shopkeeper's status and therefore less concerned with educational achievement than others, the Shimzakis nevertheless felt the old man's impatience had compromised the girl's future.

In view of the abrasive day-to-day relations within the family before his death, the change in the survivors' behavior at the funeral and later was remarkable. Feelings of affection that had been left unexpressed welled up suddenly. Before the coffin was carried out of the house for cremation, each family member, as is customary, came up to take a symbolic stroke at driving the first nail into the lid. Although the granddaughter had managed to maintain her composure up to this point, when her turn came she suddenly broke and ran from the room to hide her tears.

On a visit to the house several days later, I found conversation turning frequently to the old man and his habits. His radio remained on the kitchen table as a reminder of his absence—family members had identified him so strongly with it they had wanted to place it in his coffin "so he won't get lonely," bending only under protest to the undertaker's explanation that this was against the crematorium's regulations. It was mid-January, the time of the first sumo tournament of the year, and the television screen filled with huge human forms straining for advantage until one finally drove the other from the ring. The outcome of one match brought a comment from Ken'ichi, Keisuke's son and successor in the family business: "Grandfather must be happy because Takanohana won today." Takanohana, an immensely popular wrestler at the time, had been the old man's favorite.

"You remember how much he liked Takanohana. He could never stand to watch him wrestle because he hated to see him lose. You'd tell him [since with his bad eyes he could no longer distinguish the wrestlers' names or faces on the screen], 'Grandfather, it's Takanohana's turn next,' and he'd get up and go to the toilet. He'd come back after it was over and ask who had won." As the others smiled at this familiar image, it was plain the old man's shortcomings had already become less distinct in their memories than these pleasant quirks and idiosyncrasies.

Just as the dead man's faults were forgotten soon after his funeral, so the frictions that constantly arise between parents and children are overlooked in the wedding. What remains is the ideal image created by the suppression of the less-laudable aspects of an individual's personality in one instance, and of a social relationship in the other. Both images thus resemble the wedding's idealized image of the husband/wife relationship: all are selective distortions of real life, whether of something about to begin or something already ended. All images of this sort help to maintain the illusion of a more perfect order in life, an illusion that is celebrated in isolated moments like the wedding or the prayer at the family grave or altar. But to maintain this illusion the Japanese need not one but two kinds of distortion, two ways of seeing that are both conveniently incomplete. One holds up an image as if to say: "This is the way it will be; it will be good." The other counters: "Yes, that's the way it was; it was nice."

The emotional power of the flower presentation points to an explanation still more directly related to the ideal of adult status. For a Japanese the image of one's parents, and the sacrifices they made in raising one from childhood, is the most powerful reminder of the individual's dependence on others for his very existence. Indeed it is used as such to induce an awareness of the incompleteness of the person, as seen in Kondo's account of a weeklong ethics training seminar to which she and fellow company employees were sent "as part of an effort to make us better human beings—hence, better workers" (1982: 9). The daily regimen of lectures, exercise, and meditation stressed, among other things, cultivating a sense of gratitude to one's parents: "Recall, said the teacher, the faces of your father and mother when they saw you off; their faces when they took care of you when you were sick" (p. 26). For one particularly difficult session, in which the participants were forced to sit bare-legged on top of a layer of gravel, they were admonished "that the pain . . . is only one ten-thousandth of the pain that our mothers felt in bearing us" (p. 32). While the theme of indebtedness to parents was not the only one stressed in the program, Kondo found it astonishingly moving for the participants. Surely its inclusion was calculated to contribute to the program's goal of enhancing "individual and group happiness" by increasing awareness of "the connectedness of the self to others" (p. 52).

A similar use of the parental image to promote an awareness

of the interrelation with others is found in a psychiatric technique called Naikan therapy. Described as "a form of guided introspection," Naikan therapy is credited, among other things, with the ability to promote the patient's "realization of his responsibility for his social role(s)." To this end the patient is urged to reflect on the "memories of the care and benevolence you have received from a particular person, . . . what you have returned to that person, [and] the troubles and worries you have given that person." The patient routinely begins by considering his relationship with his mother, and then continues with other family members (Murase 1974: 431–34).

In similar fashion the flower presentation reminds the couple of the hardships their parents endured for their benefit, and the pain they as children caused in return. "In order to raise me as a child," declares one of the standard narrations used at White Crane Palace, "having to labor over and over again, surely there were nights when you could not sleep." A bride who wrote her own narration recalled her parents' concern during her hospitalization as but one of the many times "when I caused you to worry, when I was scolded or praised; there is no end to such memories." Surely these images help cultivate in the newlyweds an awareness of their incompleteness as persons, and contribute thereby to the wedding's task of depicting the ideal condition of adulthood in Japan. For who can deny, when confronted with such powerful reminders of parental pain and sacrifice, the debt one owes others for one's own existence? Who dares to assert that he is truly his own man, able to survive alone and not by the grace of others?

Indeed, who could be so selfish?

Conclusion

"What they've done, you see, is skillfully exploit the yearning for stardom."

This reply to my question about the reasons for the commercial wedding industry's success came from a priest at Hirayama's largest Shinto shrine. True, part of that success is due to other factors, he conceded. The industry, for instance, has met the customers' need for larger facilities for the reception, since the current average of more than 65 guests far exceeds the capacity of most modern homes. But he kept returning to the commercialized wedding's sumptuousness as the source of its appeal.

"The younger generation has grown up in front of the TV set," he noted. "They've been continually exposed to its visual celebration of stardom. The wedding industry now offers them a chance to star in an elaborate production, if just for one day." Of course other factors the priest did not mention have contributed to the wedding industry's growth. One is the importance now placed on the interests of the principals, whose friends and company associates are routinely invited to the wedding and account for most of the increase in the number of guests. Another is the country's general economic prosperity, which has made possible both the wedding's larger size and its greater sumptuousness. Yet another is the convenience of receiving a wide range of services through a single organization.

But none of these factors, including the attraction of stardom, can explain the specific form those services have come to take. As I hope I have shown, an additional factor behind the popularity of the commercialized wedding is nothing other than the industry's ability to provide services that contribute to the wedding as a rite of passage. The cake-cutting ceremony, the candle service, and the flower presentation all draw on basic values to image ideals regarding the new status of the principals, both as husband and wife and as adult members of society. Together these services provide the answer to the first of two historical issues raised in the introduction: the relation between the wedding's commercialization and its symbolic content. For far from distorting the wedding's function as a rite of passage—that of stating basic values—the industry has exploited that function by devising commercial services that fulfill it in a symbolically coherent fashion.

But if this process has contributed to the wedding's widespread acceptance, it argues more generally that the symbolic realm of cultural meanings constrains the possible directions of, and thereby outlines the strategy for, the commercial development of ritual. In support of this thesis I now examine another aspect of the link between the cultural realm and the wedding's commercialization. I argue that the structure of the wedding, as it has evolved in the hands of commercial specialists, successfully solves practical problems of its performance by drawing on a fundamental aspect of Japanese culture: its most characteristic approach to experience.

The Wedding as a Series of Poses

I begin with an embellishment on the cake-cutting ceremony that I observed at White Crane Palace. It was only an experiment, one of many attempts the wedding hall makes to add new elements, most of which in fact do not end up being incorporated permanently into the ceremony. It is instructive nonetheless, for it represents the extreme application—in this case probably too extreme to catch on—of a principle central to the wedding hall's structuring of both this event and the wedding as a whole.

The embellishment centers on a machine installed in one of White Crane Palace's reception rooms: a circular platform about a foot high and four and a half feet around, just large enough to hold the bride and the groom, plus the cake on its cylindrical stand, powered by an electric motor that rotates the platform slowly 140 degrees in one direction, stops, and then rotates it back the other way. Employees explained that the intent was to give everyone a good view of the ceremony and a chance to take a picture of the newlyweds from the proper angle as they maintain their pose with the knife inserted in the cake. It would also help prolong the event, making it more memorable and more satisfying for the customers.

The platform is accordingly the logical extension of the wedding industry's general concern for creating a memorable occasion by drawing the action into a pose and highlighting that pose with the spotlight, the background music, and the narration. This concern is quite plausibly grounded in conventions of traditional Japanese theater. As a key element in Kabuki, for example, an actor will strike and maintain a dramatic pose, or *mie*, which "like a visual exclamation point . . . momentarily halts the action of the play and intensifies its emotion. *Mie* is held for several seconds (the better the actor, the longer it can be held), then is gradually relaxed, and the play continues" (Brandon 1978: 84). In similar fashion the posing in the wedding can be seen as a conventional way of focusing attention on an emotional high point of the performance.

I believe the intensity found in such dramatic poses depends, however, on a basic Japanese approach to experience that is hardly limited to dramatic conventions. It consists of a tendency to separate experience into discrete contexts, isolated from each other as well as from the temporal flow, and to focus on each context, sphere, or pose as a gestalt, a thing unto itself. My observations on this general mode of cognition draw largely from Benedict's analysis of Japanese morality, which deserves paraphrasing here.[1] Benedict described Japanese social life as compartmentalized spheres of activity, each with its own code of conduct, each complete in itself. She held that the Japanese, unlike Westerners, had little concern for integrating these separate spheres into more consistent wholes by applying universal standards across the breadth of experience. She also pointed to the implications this difference has for views of behavior and the concept of the self. Westerners are baffled by the Japanese ability to follow separate or even conflicting standards in different situations, "to swing from one behavior to another without psychic cost." Westerners expect people to behave consistently, to bring something constant of themselves into each situation they enter, and thus order human existence by achieving a gestalt in their own characters. I can only supplement Benedict's analysis by making explicit one of its insights: for the Japanese order in existence is external, lying within the gestalt that is the property of each particular context.

Nowhere is this more evident than in the realm of social relations. For the moral argument that the person is incomplete demands that individuals embed themselves in larger relational wholes and assume the roles defined in those contexts. The view of maturity as the ability to come to terms with the demands these roles entail means, moreover, that the social context plays a large part in defining the person—larger indeed than any inherent quality the individual brings to that context. This is certainly the import of Nakane's analysis (1970: 2–3), which asserts the priority of the organizational frame—the social context—over the individual attributes of its members. Thus the Japanese worker, in dealing with people outside his company, "is inclined to give precedence to institution over kind of occupation. Rather than saying, 'I am a typesetter' or 'I am a filing clerk', he is likely to say, 'I am from B Publishing Group' or 'I belong to S Company.'" Hamaguchi (1985: 302) similarly characterizes the Japanese as "relational actors" whose "consciousness of self is not an abstract quality which lies within" but rather depends on, and varies with, the social context in which they are embedded.

The emphasis on individuals embedding themselves fully in a context or frame helps explain certain characteristics generally cited for Japanese aesthetics. People who do not constantly seek to reduce the particularity of a given context, by applying universal standards they bring to it, can deal more fully and directly with each moment—as the actor and audience who together fix, for a few precious seconds, on a single pose and nothing else. The same approach shapes all aesthetic genres informed by the Zen emphasis on cultivating direct, unmediated experience; the tea ceremony provides an excellent example.[2] An intense focus on the immediate context is visible in some of the more mundane activities of the Japanese as well, such as the attention to detail and concern for composition in the daily preparation of food. As a general approach to experience that contrasts with the Westerner's emphasis on constantly seeking an overriding unity in life, this focus on immediate context, I believe, enables the Japanese to confront more intensely each area of activity as a gestalt, a thing unto itself, and to appreciate more fully its own flavor and meaning.

The commercial specialist's exploitation of this tendency is not limited to the dramatic pose of the cake-cutting ceremony. Lights, music, and narration are also used in the candle service and flower presentation to focus on poses that project an ideal image of a social relationship. In like fashion the embellishment added to the bride's entrance after a change from the bridal kimono to a furisode requires the couple to hold a pose under a paper umbrella, a traditional image of togetherness.

Of course some of the things that have caused the wedding to be structured around a series of poses are not unique to Japanese culture. The systematic use of poses draws in part on the general property of rites of passage to reorient perceptions by producing ideal images with which a person or persons may be associated. The use of posing to reinforce the association is surely related to the technical means available for celebrating such images—the cameras the guests bring to take snapshots of the events. A similar concern in America for making a photographic record of weddings in fact yields similar results: weddings are structured by a series of highly standardized poses that associate the bride and groom with certain key symbols. Before the ceremony there are several prescribed photographs of the bride with her mother and the bridesmaids that focus on images of femaleness such as the bridal gown. The groom is photographed with his father and as he shakes hands with the best man. Other poses associate the couple with symbols of fertility and prosperity: the groom and the bride together holding her bouquet, the couple as they cut the wedding cake, as they exchange bites of cake, and as they exit under a shower of rice (Freese 1982: 105–42).

But the exuberance with which the Japanese engage in their posing cannot be explained through such comparisons, as though what they do is simply the analogue of our own practices. If we too make our brides and grooms pose as they cut the cake, it is not for a full minute, or atop a rotating pedestal so all the guests can get a better view. Though things like this strike some Western observers as extreme to the point of unreasonableness, they make sense in a culture that tends, in so much of its social life, to isolate experience into discrete units, and especially, to dwell on and appreciate these units, contexts, poses, as things unto themselves. If the wedding industry has exploited the yearning for stardom, as the Shinto priest asserts, its strategy for doing so has equally exploited an approach to experience that is fundamental to Japanese culture itself.

A more practical consideration has contributed to the structure of the wedding as a series of poses. Unlike doctors or other specialists consulted for their expertise, the commercial specialist is not the one who actually performs the role that he alone knows best. It is the principals themselves who star in the events that celebrate their day as bride and groom. The commercial specialist manipulates the lights and music, and provides the props and other staging devices used to highlight these images. Beyond this he can only instruct the principals in their roles beforehand and provide cues during the performance itself. His position is made even more difficult by a desire he shares with them for a smooth performance that will make their actions seem natural and unprompted. This alone would make complex action problematic, but it is especially so because the wedding industry forgoes the rehearsal common in the West. The concentration of weddings in certain seasons and their tendency to pile up on specific days virtually preclude the practice.

The strategy the commercial specialist adopts instead is to minimize action on the one hand and to work explicit cues unobtrusively into the performance on the other. The best example of cueing at work is found in the exaggerated movements of the miko as they guide the couple through the complexities of the *san-san-ku-do*, the ring exchange, and the presentation of tamagushi. Consider how the groom is "instructed" to begin the *sake* exchange. The miko holding the tray raises it chest high and, arms fully extended, advances a step toward the groom as the signal for him to pick up the first cup. She then lowers the tray and steps back, and the other miko now raises the vessel holding the *sake* and comes forward, indicating her intention to pour it. She too steps back after she pours the *sake*, leading to the only difficult moment in the ceremony. Neither the miko nor the employee who directs the ceremony has any way of instructing the groom in his next move short of saying "Drink!" and shattering the solemnity of the performance. Fortunately most grooms need no cue at this point, although I observed one flustered young man look inquiringly at the miko and twice whisper "Drink?" before responding to her nods of assent.

I came to appreciate the commercial specialist's skillful use of precise cueing, and his concern for the visual integrity of the performance, by observing a wedding that lacked both. The bride and groom were members of the Sōka Gakkai, and the ceremony was conducted by the priest of their Buddhist temple. The key difference between this wedding and the typical White Crane Palace affair was not that it lacked a commercial dimension, but rather that the business arrangement played no part in defining the relationship between the priest as provider of the service and the bride and groom as his customers. In the wedding industry the status of the customer is clearly elevated, as the director makes plain by graciously cueing the newlyweds throughout the reception with low bows and outstretched arm, showing them to their proper places on their entrance and helping them perform the cake-cutting, candle service, and so forth. Most priests, however, feel that they are religious leaders, and that as such, they stand a cut above their parishioners, despite their financial dependence on them.

This priest was no exception, and his failure to assume the secular role of stage director led to several embarrassing moments. For the *san-san-ku-do* the priest first approached the bride and then, with a tray of *sake* cups in one hand and a vessel full of *sake* in the other, stood holding both equally distant from her. She hesitated, uncertain whether to pick up the topmost cup immediately or wait for the priest to fill it first. Although he had clearly failed to communicate his intentions either verbally or through his gestures, he continued to stand motionless in front of her and made no attempt to help. Finally realizing that he would do nothing until she moved first, she took an empty cup, into which the priest then poured the *sake*. Similar miscues occurred in the ring exchange. After announcing the event, the priest merely stood by and left the couple to fend for themselves. For several moments the groom hesitated, then realizing that he had been left to act on his own initiative, he reached over to take the bride's ring from the box in front of him. Since she was seated several feet away, he rose and stepped to his left, bending over to place it on her finger. Now the groom faced an extremely awkward moment. The bride had remained seated, weighted down by her heavy robes and headdress, and the box with the groom's ring was clearly out of her reach. After another moment's hesitation, the young man arrived at the most practical, although somewhat incongruous, solution. Reaching over, he plucked his own ring from the box and passed it to the bride, then extended his hand for her to place it on his finger.

The priest had plainly given little thought to the mechanics of a performance in which the main role fell to actors following an unwritten and unfamiliar script. A priest has little reason to concern himself with such matters, however, since most of his income derives from funerary and related services. Moreover, the quality of the performance has no bearing on the volume of his wedding business, which is based solely on religious affiliation. But the commercial specialist is directly affected by his customers' impressions of the ceremony. Accordingly he has great concern for the visual impact of the performance and is keenly aware of the pitfalls presented by actors who do not know their roles.

In the circumstances, it is no doubt easier for the commercial specialist to structure events so that action is held to a minimum. He has managed to do this for the events he has introduced into the wedding while still heightening their visual impact. His solution has been to develop those events in a form in which the principals' minimal actions offer him the maximum opportunity for using his own skills at highlighting and staging. He has thus successfully devised a performance that is practical in its execution, yet familiar to its audience in its approach to experience as a series of intensely savored moments. This has also permitted him to emphasize the symbolic aspects of the images thus held and admired—through both visual imagery and the spoken word (or more specifically, the narrative script and introductory speeches he supplies). These are elements to which the specialist indeed gives careful attention, for without the symbolic ability to articulate commonly held values, the poses would lack power and appeal, no matter how visually stunning.

Japan and Modernity

The second historical question raised in the introduction was to what extent Japanese values may have changed over the postwar period, specifically those regarding the place of the individual. Once again the answer has been provided by the analysis of the preceding chapters, which I briefly summarize here. In so doing I also consider an implication of this question, one I first encountered unexpectedly in some advice a Japanese sociologist gave me during his visit to the United States.

"What you should do," he said, on hearing my plan to study weddings, "is find some remote rural village where they still have the *real* wedding, the kind held in the home."

The frequency with which I heard this kind of comment as I was beginning my research in Japan made me wonder about my own past experience there: none of the half dozen weddings I had attended in as many years were home celebrations. Surely there are millions of Japanese who have never seen the "real" wedding either—are their lives any less real, or in any sense less genuinely Japanese, for that reason? To claim so would be to accede to a logic never far removed from considerations of Japan's modernity: if the real Japan lies somewhere in the remote past (or in isolated places where the past presumably survives intact), then its modern condition must bear witness to a process by which it has become less Japanese and hence, we can only conclude, more Western.

The prospect that modernization would indeed promote a society "which differs from none of the Western industrial societies more than they differ from each other" (Dore 1958: 5) was heightened with the adoption of the postwar Constitution and the Civil Code of 1948. By eliminating the official status of the ie and guaranteeing personal autonomy, these legal changes raised expectations that the autonomous individual would eventually replace the ie in cultural values as well. The ie had been the basic unit of prewar society in two respects. It was the smallest viable social unit, since individuals were always considered members of an ie—either that of their birth or one they entered through marriage or adoption. The ie was also the microcosmic representation of the larger society, encapsulating basic principles for organizing social relations in general. In requiring the

individual to subordinate his interests to those of the larger collectivity and to accept his proper station in a hierarchically
ordered whole, the ie had ideally served the needs of the Meiji
government, standing as a metaphor for the supremacy of the
state over the individual citizen. Moreover, the continuity of the
ie—as a single social unit persisting across generations—enabled
all of society to be imaged in terms of hierarchically integrated
lines of descent branching from that of the imperial household,
which claimed genealogical seniority by virtue of its antiquity.
The traditional Confucian virtue of filial piety thus became a convenient vehicle for both expressing and exacting civic duty.

While the legal definition of the household no longer extends
across generations, most families of course continue to be concerned about the care of aging parents, a problem that is still
solved mainly through co-residence with a married child. But
even when such concerns are strongly expressed, the emphasis
in marriage has shifted to the needs of the principals rather than
those of their families. Nevertheless, it is not as individuals that
their interests hold priority, for the conclusion of this work can
only be that the individual has not replaced the ie as the fundamental unit in cultural values, despite the legal changes. Rather,
the katei has become its successor—particularly in its minimal
form as the husband/wife relationship, for here we see most
clearly the katei meeting the two criteria set out earlier: it is the
smallest viable social unit, and it is a microcosm for the larger
society. As the husband/wife relationship alone, the katei is
both the smallest social unit and the requirement for gaining recognition as fully adult. It also expresses most economically the
basic principle that the person is incomplete: husbands and
wives lack competencies ascribed to their opposites, hence individuals need to enter into interdependent relations with others
in order to get along in the world.

Moreover, the husband/wife unit as depicted in the wedding
is both hierarchically ordered—again because of differences ascribed to men and women—and harmonious. Here too the katei's aspect of microcosm is most economically expressed, for not
only are these characteristics shared more generally by the family, but the qualities of harmonious cooperation between members of a hierarchically ordered whole are held to extend to

organizational contexts in the larger society—such as modern corporations, for which the family is often taken explicitly as model. In the many examinations we have of Japanese companies (e.g., Abegglen 1958; Clark 1979; Nakane 1970; Rohlen 1974), we see most plainly the continuity with prewar values, for it is with the ie that the metaphor of firm-as-family is frequently expressed.

Thus while the legal form of the ie has been abolished, its underlying principles of hierarchy and harmonious interdependence—principles that inevitably deny the autonomy of the individual—survive in its successor as basic unit. If this continuity shows a remarkable conservatism in the values of contemporary Japan, it is surely because the coherence of those values constitutes an argument for how life ought to be lived that is as compelling in the modern world as it was in the past—an argument that is no less Japanese today for all its modernity.

Reference Material

Notes

Introduction

1. This pseudonym draws on the long-standing use of the crane—a symbol for longevity and happiness—as a wedding motif. In like manner, the names of modern wedding halls frequently incorporate themes and images traditionally associated with marriage ceremonies.

2. My stint allowed me to observe 20 wedding receptions in their entirety and substantial portions of a dozen more. During my year of research I also observed the more highly standardized wedding ceremony eight times—six at White Crane Palace and twice elsewhere.

3. Strictly speaking, this authority was exercised by parents or guardians to age 30 for men and 25 for women (Sebald 1934: 176). In the prewar years, however, men and women typically entered into their first marriage before reaching these ages (Mosk 1980; Taeuber 1958: 225).

4. The promulgation of the Civil Code did not terminate this debate, however, for Meiji ideological discourse, as Gluck (1985) thoroughly documents, was a far looser and more gradual process than has been generally recognized. For more specific discussion of the prewar status of the ie and the postwar legal changes affecting it, see Dore (1958: 91–120), Steiner (1950), Wagatsuma (1950), and Watanabe (1963).

5. Studies in which the incidence of or the attitudes toward ren'ai and miai marriage are seen as indexes of a change in values include Baber (1958), Blood (1967), Steiner (1950), Vogel (1961), Wagatsuma and DeVos (1962), and Yamamuro (1960).

6. I believe the sample satisfied my aims, though it is admittedly small: a total of 30 couples, 16 of whom married within the two years prior to my fieldwork. This largely reflects my own preference for participation in Japanese social life, as opposed to the distance of the formal interview.

Chapter One

1. At White Crane Palace the size of the shrine room limits the maximum attendance at the Shinto ceremony to 34 people, typical for establishments of the wedding industry. A priest of the largest Shinto shrine in Hirayama blames the small size of such facilities for the current trend to invite only close relatives to the ceremony. He was quick to point out that his shrine has always allowed as many as possible to attend, and that groups of 70 or more are not uncommon.

2. Occasionally two sets of nakōdo are used at the ceremony, one chosen by the bride's family and one by the groom's. However, the presence of a second set does not significantly alter the content or sequence of events as described in this chapter.

3. All four are full-time employees of the wedding hall. The priests have received religious training and certification from the Shinto shrine with which White Crane Palace is affiliated, but the miko are office workers who ordinarily perform no other religious functions and have received no special training outside the wedding hall.

4. There are a number of variations of this ceremony, however, and an equally large number of alternate explanations for the name. According to Hendry's (1981: 174) informants, the correct sequence for the exchange is as follows: the bride, the groom, then the bride drink from the first cup, the groom, the bride, then the groom drink from the second, and then back to the original order for the third, or a total of nine drinks from the three cups. I observed this sequence performed in a Buddhist wedding ceremony conducted by a priest of the Sōka Gakkai sect.

5. Flattering introductions like these are sometimes hard to make. Nobody's life story is without shortcomings, and some contain more than others. The speaker's usual response in such cases is to remain silent rather than jeopardize the wedding's image of the couple as ideal. For example, the lengthy detail about the couple's scholastic achievements and employment records in this speech contrasts sharply with the introduction given the bride in another wedding I observed: "The bride, Tomoko, was born on October 16, 1957, as the eldest daughter of Yanagimoto Fumiko of Shimoda-chō in Hirayama. From the time she graduated from Hirayama Women's High School, she has applied herself diligently to the study of domestic skills [hanayome shugyō] in preparation for this wonderful day." The lack of specific information about the bride's activities for the six years that had elapsed since high school was deliberate. The phrase "the study of domestic skills" ordinarily refers to training in a broad range of activities felt to increase a woman's value as a bride, including the traditional arts of flower arranging, tea

ceremony, and calligraphy, as well as cooking and sewing. Many women study one or more of these arts at some point before marriage, a fact often noted in the nakōdo's introduction as a praiseworthy achievement. In this case, however, the nakōdo was using the term to cover up something he preferred not to mention: that the bride's mother ran a bar where the bride had been working since leaving school. Also noteworthy is the attempt to gloss over the bride's parents' divorce by using only her mother's name. Both divorce and a young woman's working in a bar are topics that require discretion under ordinary circumstances; they are hardly information a nakōdo wishes to include about the bride in his introduction of her as the embodiment of society's ideals.

6. It is considered improper to use the word "cut" at weddings because of its occurrence in a metaphor for the severing of social relations (*en o kiru*—lit., "cut the connection"). Hence the emcee here introduces the act of cutting with the phrase "inserting the knife"; I discuss a similar circumlocution in Chap. 5. The taboo is not strictly observed, however. Recall the passage from the shuhin's speech quoted above: "Today's wedding is the emergence of a new flower. The future will bring both warm winds to make it bloom and cold winds that cut at the roots."

7. "Asobi" can have a variety of meanings, including the perfectly innocuous senses of amusement and recreation (Smith and Wiswell 1982: 111). Here it is used to suggest dissipation, in deliberate contrast with the words of praise the speaker has just uttered.

8. It is of course more realistic when the bride and groom write the text themselves, supplying details of events from their own lives. But when they do, they tend to echo the themes of the wedding hall's standard versions. One bride's speech resembles the text example in describing her parents' joy at her birth, but she supplements it with an image of their subsequent suffering and care.

> All of a sudden this day has come. Born the last of four children, it was Father who named me Keiko ["blessing child"] since he was finally blessed with a girl. It was Mother who felt happy to see tiny red clothes floating among the laundry.
>
> When I was hospitalized last October and returned to my room after the operation, it was Mother and Father who were waiting for me, looking worriedly at my face to see if I was all right. The times when I caused you to worry, when I was scolded, comforted, and praised; there is no end to such memories. Thank you for raising me these twenty-four years, without regard for my being a girl or a boy.
>
> Although my name will change from Moriyama to Tanaka, I will always remain your daughter. Thank you truly.

Chapter Two

1. For this account I have relied generally on Ema's (1971) history of wedding customs; more specific information on samurai schools of etiquette was obtained from Ogasawara (1967) and on Heian weddings and marriage practices from Ikeda (1964) and McCullough (1967).

2. This reputation is specific to the matchmaking role; it does not attach to the ceremonial nakōdo who appears in the wedding.

3. However, the folklorists' attempt to fit all variants into a single evolutionary framework of change from matrilocality to patrilocality has proved unconvincing. This framework was borrowed in the early 20th century from the work of Lewis Henry Morgan (e.g., *Ancient Society*; 1877). Although now discredited in the West, his views have enjoyed a surprising degree of influence in Japan. See Seki (1958: 170) and Uematsu (1978: 31–36).

4. This form of marriage is a variant of what Yanagita (1957: 162–63) describes as *ashiirekon*, a form of trial marriage. Lebra (1984: 106, 319) too has found evidence that this form of marriage was common in the early decades of the century; and Emori (1986: 30) reports an instance of ashiirekon as recently as 1961.

5. The trip to the groom's house (some 20 km away) was made in a bus chartered for the occasion; Embree (1939: 207) reports that bus transport had become common practice in rural Kyushu as well by the mid-1930s. Formerly brides walked. My informant's 95-year-old father, who was present at the interview, remembered some journeys of as much as 10 kilometers. It was quite common for the hem of the bride's kimono to be frayed and worn by the end of the trip. See also Lebra (1984: 107).

6. This account of the origins of the gojokai system is based on Zengoren sanjūnenshi henshū iinkai (1978).

7. It is not clear whether the gojokai company at first actually paid for the catering and other services provided by outside establishments, or whether the members bore these costs, as is currently the case, with the gojokai merely acting as broker in securing services on their behalf. The latter arrangement offers financial benefits nonetheless, since the gojokai's volume of business enables it to bargain for special rates for its members.

8. Although gojokai companies have continued to provide funerary services for their members, for the remainder of this account I describe only developments related to wedding services and facilities.

9. One result of this growth has been greater organizational complexity. By the end of the 1970s the original Gojokai had split into a number of different companies, all members of a larger organization

known as the Hirayama Gojokai Group. White Crane Palace is run as a separate company belonging to this group, as is a similar facility constructed for funerary services. Other member companies include one that continues to operate the original gojokai plan, now concentrating solely on its enrollment program; and a business and accounting office that oversees the finances of all the other companies. Despite these changes the Gojokai Group is essentially a continuation of the company founded by Ishida Tsuyoshi, who maintains control over its operation. For simplicity I continue to refer to the entire organization as the Hirayama Gojokai.

10. Rising wedding costs long ago forced the organization to abandon some of its original benefits, which included, for example, the free use of bridal robes owned by the Gojokai. Current rental prices for the robes alone range from ¥60,000 to ¥500,000 ($250 to $2,083); a gojokai member who selects one costing ¥250,000 may receive a discount of up to half the price.

11. Ema (1971: 215) reports that hotels were used for receptions even in the prewar period. But in Hirayama it was only after the opening of White Crane Palace that hotels began to aggressively cultivate such business. First-class hotels charge more than wedding halls for the same type of service, and informants assert that this higher price is commanded in part by the hotel's reputation alone. White Crane Palace is hampered in its attempt to compete with these establishments on equal terms because of its association with the gojokai system, whose original purpose of providing low-cost ceremonies still gives the facility a plebeian image in the minds of many.

12. As a private business, of course, the Gojokai has always had profit as one of its goals, maintained in conjunction with its more openly expressed ideology of serving the common good. Informants long associated with the organization assert, however, that the founder was sincerely dedicated to this ideology in the early years.

13. Lebra (1984: 110) comments on this trend, for example, and cites a case that suggests its roots go back to the late 1950s.

14. This comparative commercialization of weddings held in public facilities was true for one wedding I attended in the mid-1970s, and another one held by an informant in 1982. And indeed the Sanwa data suggest the same thing, since only six of 410 couples reported conspicuously low expenditures (under ¥500,000) on their ceremony and reception. The majority of the approximately 60 couples who used public facilities, then, were paying sums comparable to those charged by commercial establishments, and presumably for comparable services.

15. Services for the reception are provided by commercial enterprises under contract with the shrine, not by the shrine itself.

16. The only other pattern that might be numerically significant is not indicated in the Sanwa data: that of having a reception at an ordinary restaurant, in conjunction with some form of ceremony elsewhere or with no ceremony at all. One couple I interviewed had a restaurant reception, but I doubt whether this example represents more than a few percent of all weddings nowadays.

17. The Gojokai has played a considerable role in this expansion of the urban pattern by undertaking to enroll families in rural areas in its prepayment system long before they have any need for wedding services.

18. Hendry (1981: 171–72) reports a similar mixture of traditional and commercial services for rural Kyushu in the mid- to late 1970s.

Chapter Three

1. This applied mostly to marriages involving younger adults; Smith and Wiswell (1982: 153) note that "older men and women frequently made their own arrangements." General accounts of prewar miai marriage are found in Embree (1939) and Dore (1958). Smith and Wiswell (1982) give the most detailed account of actual marriage arrangements and of the overall shape of relations between the sexes for the prewar period, although they deal only with rural society.

2. Blood therefore divided his sample into four groups (pure miai, qualified miai, qualified ren'ai, pure ren'ai) based on informants' verbal replies to the question: "In general, would you classify your marriage as a miai marriage or a love match?" In only 61% of the cases did the husband and wife agree on the status of their marriage using this fourfold classification. From his data, however, it appears the figure would be 90% if the sample were divided into just the two groups of miai and ren'ai.

3. In rural areas, however, concern about a marriage's effect on the family's status still promotes a more thorough investigation of the prospective mate's background (Hendry 1981: 133–38).

4. One study shows that miai marriages made up 40% of the nationwide total in 1977 (NHK hōsō yoron chōsajo 1980: 271). The Sanwa Bank survey found only 24% of its urban white-collar sample married by miai.

5. This applies to most of the sects generally known as the New Religions, and especially to the largest of them, the Sōka Gakkai.

6. See Lebra's (1984: 84–86) discussion of the disadvantages faced by women who must seek in-marrying husbands. The personnel at White Crane Palace always ascertain whether a marriage is a *muko-tori* affair, since it is then the bride's parents who handle the financial negotiations. Of the 228 weddings in my sample, only 11 (4.8%) were *muko-tori*.

7. These services divide into two types: those operated by municipal

governments for the public benefit, which are usually free of charge, and those operated as private businesses. Commercial incentive makes private organizations more aggressive in their pursuit of clients and perhaps less selective in their recommendations for a match, but the procedure for both types is the same.

8. For many women who pursue teaching as a career, remaining single is an acceptable option, though hardly preferable.

9. In fact the yuinō frequently serves as the occasion for decisions on the date and place of the wedding, because it is usually the first time after the miai that the couple, their parents, and the nakōdo all meet together.

10. These occasions, called *chugen* and *oseibo*, come in early summer and late December, respectively.

11. There were 20 uncles and 13 company superiors for a combined total of 72%. "Company superiors" was defined broadly to include, for example, the school principal of Takagi Akiko in Case 5. An additional seven nakōdo were other kinds of relatives: three cousins, two brothers-in-law, and two identified simply as "relative." The other six included a neighbor, a family acquaintance, two men who had served as nakōdo for the groom's parents, and a man identified simply as the groom's *onshi*, someone to whom the groom owed a debt of gratitude.

12. The Takagis had two sets of nakōdo, one representing each family. Most informants considered this the older and more proper thing to do, but it is by no means clear that the practice was ever universal. In most cases I observed, no particular reason was given; it was simply regarded as a matter of choosing the more formal of two equally acceptable alternatives. In the Takagis' case, I was told that the brides' parents insisted on the second set because they felt that if there should ever be any trouble in which a nakōdo would be called in to mediate, Akiko would be at a disadvantage if the only nakōdo was a relative of the groom. Akiko thought her parents' fears were groundless but went along with the request.

Chapter Four

1. Strictly speaking, the term yuinō denotes the payment or exchange that formalizes the betrothal; *yuinō hin* and *yuinō kin* are the betrothal gifts and the cash payment made on the occasion of the *yuinō shiki*, the ceremony proper. I follow the practice of using yuinō alone, as in everyday Japanese, to indicate, depending on context, the exchange, the gifts or cash payment, or the ceremony.

2. Ideally, the full complement for the yuinō is the nakōdo, the couple, and the parents. The nakōdo's wife may or may not attend, but if any of the others do not come, it is for compelling reasons. In one

case I encountered, the nakōdo did not attend due to a sudden illness; in another the couple was not there because they could not accommodate their work schedules to those of their parents. The ceremony may be held somewhere other than the bride's home, but again only if there is substantial reason. A restaurant was used in one instance because the nakōdo was a man of particularly prominent status, and the bride's home was felt to be too ordinary a setting.

3. The Sanwa Bank survey indicates the current popularity of these practices in urban areas. Yuinō payments were made in 87% of the cases in the sample, with return payments of cash made in 43%. Engagement rings and similar non-cash items were given by 89% of the grooms; and 57% of the brides made return gifts.

4. A detailed account of these items is found in Hendry (1981: 159–60).

5. Formerly it was common for return gifts of lesser value to be made to the groom's family, either when the yuinō payment was made or when the bride went to the groom's home for the wedding ceremony. The idea of return gifts survives in both forms. In one instance I observed a return cash payment made to the groom's party at the yuinō ceremony. Although the gifts exchanged took the same form, cash, the envelopes specified the traditional uses for such funds: "obi money" for the bride and "*hakama* (a part of the traditional men's formal attire) money" for the groom. Even when no immediate return payment is made, the notion of exchange is implicit in the view that the money given to the bride is for preparations for the wedding and married life. It is recognized, moreover, that the items she brings in her trousseau usually equal or surpass the yuinō in value. This was reason enough for one groom not to regret the payment, explaining that "it all comes back as furniture anyway."

6. In the Sanwa survey, for example, fewer than 1% of the weddings took place in one or other of the summer months of July and August, with another 4% in June. December and January accounted for only 2% and 8%, respectively. The bulk of the sample was split between the spring and fall seasons, with 46% occurring between February and May, and 40% between September and November.

7. The sequence of designations is Senshō (also called Sakigachi), Tomobiki, Senbu (also Sakimake), Butsumetsu, Taian (also Daian), and Shakku.

8. Appropriate days are impossible for the ordinary person to predict because the situation is made still more complicated by the fact that the astrological sequence is reset to begin with a different day-designation at the beginning of each lunar month of the old calendar.

9. At White Crane Palace, 33% of the wedding receptions over a

12-month period were held on the 14 Taian or Tomobiki Sundays and holidays occurring in the spring (February–May) and fall (late September–early December) seasons. An additional 29% occurred on the 16 Sundays or holidays during those periods that are considered neutral.

10. The arrangements for the trip, including the wedding ceremony (conducted in Japanese) at a church in Honolulu, were made by a travel agent in Hirayama. Since the couple went by themselves, personnel in Hawaii performed the necessary roles of witnessing the marriage and giving away the bride.

11. The full itinerary takes the party from the bridal robes; to smaller display of furisode, the other formal kimono the bride may wear during the reception; to the photographer's corner, to select the number and types of formal poses to be taken in the wedding hall's studios; to a display of Western formal dresses for the bride to wear during the last part of the reception; and finally to displays of hikidemono items and wax models of the food for the reception. Customers also decide at this point on the inclusion of such events as the cake-cutting ceremony and the candle service. The groom then examines formal wear he will rent for the wedding, the traditional Japanese kimono and a Western tuxedo. In the meantime the bride makes appointments for fitting the rented clothes and the wig she will wear as part of her bridal costume. The entire party then proceeds to the reservation department, where they drop off their order forms and perhaps consult about details of their decisions. Some customers then go to the travel-agency counter to inquire about honeymoon packages or make arrangements for visas and accommodations.

12. The standard set of courses ranges from 8 dishes to the deluxe 14-dish combination; 75% of the customers choose either the 11- or the 12-dish menu.

13. As noted earlier, the emcee may show slides of the couple, for example, beginning with shots from their infant or early childhood days, and accompany these with a lighthearted narration.

14. The Sanwa survey supports these observations to the extent that its results are applicable. Unfortunately, it combines the costs of the yuinō payment and the couple's engagement gifts, which represent the clearest opposition of familial vs. individual interests, into the single category of "betrothal expenditures." But it does show that, of the remaining expenditures, the couple bore, on the average, almost all of the cost for the honeymoon (84%) as opposed to less than half for the wedding ceremony and reception (43%). Questions about the couple's attitudes toward wedding costs support the same conclusions. Asked to name which categories incurred too much expense, the most frequent

response (28%) was the ceremony and reception. By contrast, of the categories on which couples wished they had spent more, the largest proportion named the honeymoon (21%).

Chapter Five

1. Tambiah (1968: 202) suggests that all ritual can be seen as such an attempt to "re-structure and integrate the minds and the emotions of the actors."

2. Hendry (1981: 195; citing Ema 1971: 169) reports that this popularization of the Shinto wedding began in 1898. But Ema's chronology is clearly in error: he mistakenly gives the date for the imperial wedding as Feb. 1, 1897, but then, in the same passage, correctly reports the Crown Prince's year of birth as 1879 (Aug. 31, to be exact), and his age at marriage as 20 (1971: 174).

3. Although the vast majority of weddings are Shinto—90% in the Sanwa Bank survey and 94% in the White Crane Palace sample (see Table 1)—certain groups regularly prefer a Buddhist ceremony, according to wedding-industry personnel. The most notable of these are members of the Sōka Gakkai, who normally refuse to participate in the Shinto wedding. The Buddhist wedding ceremony I briefly describe in the Conclusion involved a couple whose families belong to this sect. Because of the stigma generally attached to this group, when only one of the principals is a member, the other's family usually objects to the Buddhist ceremony. The result is typically a nonreligious ceremony conducted at a commercial wedding facility. At White Crane Palace fewer than 1% of the weddings are of this type, and 2% of the customers simply hold their wedding reception there, after being married in a Buddhist service elsewhere.

4. On separate room, Bacon (1902: 63), Dixon (1885: 16), Norbeck (1954: 183); on screened area, Embree (1939: 207), Smith (1956: 79); on attendance of only nakōdo or *sake* pourer, Kuchler (1885: 123), Inouye (1911: 183).

5. Thus the person chosen for the task of sprinkling the rice in the palanquin, according to Ema (1971: 140), was a female retainer with many descendants; also placed inside was a papier-mâché dog, an animal that was held to characteristically produce a large number of offspring and to have easy deliveries (pp. 80–81).

6. Gail Bernstein (personal communication, 1987) witnessed this practice in rural Shikoku in 1974.

Chapter Six

1. In his study of Japanese high schools, Rohlen (1983: 156) characterizes the modern curriculum of kateika "as an introduction to the

family and to household management." Classes in *kateika* are taught at all educational levels. They are taken by both boys and girls in elementary school, but beyond this by girls only.

2. This broader folk definition should be distinguished from the narrower analytic sense of shakai—visible in such applications as *shakaigaku*, "sociology," or *shihonshugi shakai*, "capitalist society"—which I do not include in this discussion.

3. For treatments of the *uchi/soto* distinction in the Western literature on Japan, see Kondo (1982), Lebra (1976), and Nakane (1970).

4. These styles of headdress are called *tsunokakushi* and *watabōshi*, respectively. The practice of keeping the head covered outside the home began as an upper-class custom in the Muromachi period (1333–1573). In the Tokugawa era (1603–1868) it was first adopted by all women of the Jōdō Shinsū Buddhist sect for visits to the temple and later came into common use for all ceremonial occasions. It now survives only in the bridal costume. The tsunokakushi (horn-hider) is variously interpreted as intended to hide the wife's "horns of jealousy" over her husband's infidelities or intended to hide a woman's bad traits from her husband to signify her obedience to him. (See Ema 1971: 80, Hendry 1981: 170, 195 n.54, and Katō 1979: 32–34.) While such folk etymologies may not accurately reflect the custom's origins, their currency attests to the pervasiveness with which wives are accorded the inferior position in public discourse.

5. If the groom has no father, an older brother or an uncle will give the speech.

6. Osako's study is valuable for its demonstration of strong attachment to the traditional images of the gender role even in the exceptional case of women who follow professional careers. These working women—especially when they are mothers—remain committed to fulfilling the role of homemaker. One prerequisite for balancing conflicting role demands is a supportive husband who is understanding and flexible about the division of labor at home. But husbands apparently cannot completely cover for their wives' domestic tasks; the majority of professional women with children rely on parents or in-laws for help in child care. More generally, professional women are also quite traditional in seeing their husbands' work as more important than their own: "They made the point very clearly that the husband's job is *extremely* important. They said they took pains not to disrupt his work performance, even at their own inconvenience. For instance, an editor in a unionized publishing firm where her husband also worked reported that when the child got sick, she stayed home until she used up all her sick leave and then her husband took over. . . . The working mothers in our sample, instead of asserting equality with the spouse,

were generally grateful to spouses generous enough to let them work" (Osako 1978: 19; emphasis in original).

7. In the Sanwa Bank survey the average groom was 27.4 years of age, had an annual income of ¥3,248,000, and had savings of ¥2,768,000 at marriage. The typical bride was 24.7 years old, had an annual income of ¥1,944,000, and had savings of ¥2,872,000.

8. For recent criticisms of the image of the Japanese as group oriented, see Befu (1980) and Mouer and Sugimoto (1986).

9. A considerable number of works on Japan have focused on these themes. There are studies of the interplay between individual lives and the cultural ideals of roles (Plath 1980); examinations of how workers, far from being complacent in their jobs, often wish to quit—but usually do not (Clark 1979; Cole 1979); investigations of women who, not content with the housewife's standard lot, seek alternatives in the bar and restaurant business that are readily available but negatively valued (Jackson 1976) or in higher-status professional careers that are far more difficult to pursue (Osako 1978; Plath 1980: 172–212); and biographies of memorable people like Bernstein's (1983) strong-willed yet disciplined Haruko, who masters her given roles so thoroughly she seems to gain control of her life without losing her critical awareness of the paths she would really have preferred to follow.

10. This detail of the ceremony is not universal, but a version of the candle service I witnessed at another wedding hall achieved the same emphasis through an alternate means. The couple entered the reception room together holding a single candle, already lit. As they went to light the candles in front of the groom's parents and then the bride's, an accompanying narration (performed by an employee of the wedding hall) emphasized the couple's debt to their parents for having raised them up to the day of their marriage, the day that marked their becoming "respectable members of society."

11. The flower presentation also differs from the other two events in minor ways. It was incorporated in the ceremonies several years earlier than the candle service and cake-cutting, and its cost is automatically included in the basic reception fee all customers pay. Both differences may be the result of longer and more intimate relations between wedding halls and florists.

12. An embellishment occasionally included in the event further argues for this possibility. Two small children, usually a niece and nephew, may be chosen to present small bouquets to the bride and groom immediately before the start of the flower presentation's regular proceedings.

13. Entrance to the more prestigious public high schools is competi-

tive and somewhat risky. Over-confident applicants who fail to get into the school of their choice may suddenly be left with no desirable alternatives from which to choose. See Rohlen (1983: 123–28).

Conclusion

1. Benedict's discussion of this topic is contained in chaps. 9 and 10 of her timeless work, *The Chrysanthemum and the Sword* (1946), and exquisitely summarized on pp. 195–97.

2. Kondo (1985) demonstrates how various symbolic aspects of the tea ceremony gradually separate participants from the realm of mundane experience, thus promoting an intense focus on the immediate content of the rite.

References Cited

Japanese names are given in Western style throughout.

Abegglen, James. 1958. *The Japanese Factory*. Glencoe, Ill.: Free Press.
Baber, Ray E. 1958. *Youth Looks at Marriage and the Family: A Study of Changing Japanese Attitudes*. Tokyo: International Christian University.
Bacon, Alice M. 1902. *Japanese Girls and Women*. Boston: Houghton Mifflin.
Befu, Harumi. 1980. "The Group Model of Japanese Society and an Alternative," *Rice University Studies*, 66(1): 169–87.
Benedict, Ruth. 1946. *The Chrysanthemum and the Sword*. Boston: Houghton Mifflin.
Bernstein, Gail. 1983. *Haruko's World: A Japanese Farm Woman and Her Community*. Stanford, Calif.: Stanford University Press.
Bestor, Theodore C. 1985. "Gendered Domains: A Commentary on Research in Japanese Studies," *Journal of Japanese Studies*, 11(1): 283–87.
Blood, Robert O. 1967. *Love Match and Arranged Marriage: A Tokyo-Detroit Comparison*. New York: Free Press.
Brandon, James R. 1978. "Form in Kabuki Acting." In James R. Brandon, William P. Malm, and Donald H. Shively, *Studies in Kabuki: Its Acting, Music, and Historical Context*. Honolulu: University Press of Hawaii.
Casal, U. A. 1940. "Some Notes on the Sakazuki and the Role of Sake Drinking in Japan," *Transactions of the Asiatic Society of Japan*, 19: 46–73.
Clark, Rodney. 1979. *The Japanese Company*. New Haven, Conn.: Yale University Press.
Cole, Robert E. 1979. *Work, Mobility, and Participation: A Comparative Study of American and Japanese Industry*. Berkeley: University of California Press.
Dixon, J. M. 1885. "Japanese Etiquette," *Transactions of the Asiatic Society of Japan*, 13: 1–21.

Dore, Ronald P. 1958. *City Life in Japan: A Study of a Tokyo Ward.* Berkeley: University of California Press.

Ema, Tsutomu. 1971. *Kekkon no rekishi* [History of marriage]. Tokyo: Yūzankaku.

Embree, John F. 1939. *Suye Mura: A Japanese Village.* Chicago: University of Chicago Press.

Emori, Itsuo. 1986. *Nihon no kon'in: sono rekishi to minzoku* [Japanese marriage: its history and folklore]. Tokyo: Kōbundō.

Freese, Pamela Rae. 1982. "Holy Matrimony: A Symbolic Analysis of the American Wedding Ritual." Ph.D. dissertation, University of Virginia.

Geertz, Clifford. 1984. "'From the Native's Point of View': On the Nature of Anthropological Understanding." In Richard A. Shweder and Robert A. LeVine, eds., *Culture Theory: Essays on Mind, Self, and Emotion.* Cambridge: Cambridge University Press.

Gluck, Carol. 1985. *Japan's Modern Myths: Ideology in the Late Meiji Period.* Princeton, N.J.: Princeton University Press.

Hamaguchi, Esyun. 1985. "A Contextual Model of the Japanese: Toward a Methodological Innovation in Japanese Studies," *Journal of Japanese Studies,* 11 (2): 289–321.

Hendry, Joy. 1981. *Marriage in Changing Japan: Community and Society.* New York: St. Martin's Press.

Iida, Eiichi, and Shū Fujioka. 1979. *Kankonsōsai no jiten* [A dictionary of ceremonial etiquette]. Tokyo: Seitōsha.

Ikeda, Kikan. 1964. *Heian chō no seikatsu to bungaku* [Life and literature of the Heian court]. Tokyo: Kadokawa shoten.

Inouye, Jukichi. 1911. *Home Life in Tokyo.* Tokyo: Tokyo Printing.

Jackson, Laura. 1976. "Bar Hostesses." In Joyce Lebra, Joy Paulson, and Elizabeth Powers, eds., *Women in Changing Japan.* Boulder, Col.: Westview Press.

Kamishima, Jirō. 1969. *Nihonjin no kekkonkan* [The Japanese view of marriage]. Tokyo: Chikuma sōsho.

Katō, Yuriko. 1979. "Kaburimono [Headgear]." In Keitarō Miyamoto, ed., *Kōza Nihon no minzoku* [Japanese folklore studies], vol. 4: *I, shoku, jū* [Clothing, food, shelter]. Tokyo: Yūseidō.

Kondo, Dorinne. 1982. "Work, Family, and the Self: A Cultural Analysis of Japanese Family Enterprise." Ph.D. dissertation, Harvard University.

———. 1985. "The Way of Tea: A Symbolic Analysis," *Man,* 20: 287–306.

Kuchler, L. W. 1885. "Marriage in Japan," *Transactions of the Asiatic Society of Japan,* 13: 114–37.

Kurita, Yasuyuki. 1978. "Urban Life Seen Through Household Possessions," *Japan Echo,* 5(4): 114–23.

Lebra, Takie Sugiyama. 1976. *Japanese Patterns of Behavior*. Honolulu: University Press of Hawaii.

———. 1984. *Japanese Women: Constraint and Fulfillment*. Honolulu: University Press of Hawaii.

McCullough, William H. 1967. "Japanese Marriage Institutions in the Heian Period," *Harvard Journal of Asiatic Studies*, 27: 103–67.

Mosk, Carl. 1980. "Nuptiality in Meiji Japan," *Journal of Social History*, 13(3): 474–89.

Mouer, Ross, and Yoshio Sugimoto. 1986. *Images of Japanese Society: A Study in the Structure of Social Reality*. London: KPI.

Murase, Takao. 1974. "Naikan Therapy." In Takie Sugiyama Lebra and William P. Lebra, eds., *Japanese Culture and Behavior: Selected Readings*. Honolulu: University Press of Hawaii.

Nakane, Chie. 1970. *Japanese Society*. Berkeley: University of California Press.

Nihon Hōsō Kyōkai hōsō yoron chōsajo. 1980. *Nihon Hōsō Kyōkai yoron chōsa shiryōshū* [Nihon Hōsō Kyōkai opinion survey materials]. Tokyo: Nihon Hōsō Kyōkai sābisu sentā.

Norbeck, Edward. 1954. *Takashima: A Japanese Fishing Community*. Salt Lake City: University of Utah Press.

Ogasawara, Kiyonobu. 1967. *Ogasawara ryū* [Ogasawara etiquette]. Tokyo: Gakueisha.

Osako, Masako Murakami. 1978. "Dilemmas of Japanese Professional Women," *Social Problems*, 26(1): 15–25.

Plath, David W. 1980. *Long Engagements: Maturity in Modern Japan*. Stanford, Calif.: Stanford University Press.

Prime Minister's Statistical Office. 1979, 1980. *Yoron chōsa nenkan* [Opinion survey yearbook]. Tokyo: Sōrifu.

Rohlen, Thomas P. 1974. *For Harmony and Strength: Japanese White-Collar Organization in Anthropological Perspective*. Berkeley: University of California Press.

———. 1983. *Japan's High Schools*. Berkeley: University of California Press.

Sanwa ginkō [Sanwa Bank]. 1982. *Kekkon zengo no suitōbo* [A ledger of wedding expenditures]. Tokyo: Sanwa ginkō gyōmu kaihatsubu.

Scott, George Ryley. 1953. *Curious Customs of Sex and Marriage*. London: Torchstream.

Sebald, W. J., tr. 1934. *The Civil Code of Japan*. London: Butterworth.

Seki, Keigo. 1958. "Nihon minzoku no rekishi" [A history of Japanese folklore studies]. In Tokuzō Ōmachi et al., eds., *Nihon minzokugaku taikei* [An outline of Japanese folklore], vol. 2. Tokyo: Heibonsha.

Shiotsuki, Yaeko. 1970. *Kankon sōsai nyūmon* [Introduction to ceremonial etiquette]. Tokyo: Kōbunsha.

Smith, Robert J. 1956. "Kurusu: A Japanese Agricultural Community." In John B. Cornell and Robert J. Smith, *Two Japanese Villages*. Ann Arbor: University of Michigan, Center for Japanese Studies, Occasional Papers No. 5.

———. 1974. *Ancestor Worship in Contemporary Japan*. Stanford, Calif.: Stanford University Press.

———. 1978. *Kurusu: The Price of Progress in a Japanese Village, 1951–1975*. Stanford, Calif.: Stanford University Press.

———. 1983. *Japanese Society: Tradition, Self, and the Social Order*. New York: Cambridge University Press.

———. 1987. "Gender Inequality in Contemporary Japan," *Journal of Japanese Studies*, 13(1): 1–25.

Smith, Robert J., and Ella Lury Wiswell. 1982. *The Women of Suye Mura*. Chicago: University of Chicago Press.

Steiner, Kurt. 1950. "Postwar Changes in the Japanese Civil Code," *Washington Law Review*, 25(3): 286–312.

Taeuber, Irene B. 1958. *The Population of Japan*. Princeton, N.J.: Princeton University Press.

Tambiah, S. J. 1968. "The Magical Power of Words," *Man*, n.s. 3(2): 175–208.

Turner, Victor. 1967. "Betwixt and Between: The Liminal Period in *Rites de Passage*." In Victor Turner, *The Forest of Symbols: Aspects of Ndembu Ritual*. Ithaca, N.Y.: Cornell University Press.

Uematsu, Akashi. 1978. "Kon'inshi no mondaiten" [Problems in the study of the history of marriage]. In *Kōza Nihon no minzoku* [Japanese folklore studies], vol. 3. Tokyo: Yūseidō.

United Nations. 1977, 1983. *Demographic Yearbook* for 1976, 1981. New York: United Nations.

Van Gennep, Arnold. 1960. *The Rites of Passage*. Chicago: University of Chicago Press.

Vogel, Ezra F. 1961. "The Go-Between in a Developing Society: The Case of the Japanese Marriage Arranger," *Human Organization*, 20(3): 112–20.

Wagatsuma, Hiroshi, and George DeVos. 1962. "Attitudes Towards Marriage in Rural Japan," *Human Organization*, 21(8): 187–200.

Wagatsuma, Sakae. 1950. "Democratization of the Family Relation in Japan," *Washington Law Review*, 25(4): 405–26.

Watanabe, Yozo. 1963. "The Family and the Law: The Individualistic Premise and Modern Japanese Family Law." In Arthur Taylor von Mehren, ed., *Law in Japan: The Legal Order in a Changing Society*. Cambridge, Mass.: Harvard University Press.

Westermarck, Edward. 1926. *A Short History of Marriage*. New York: Macmillan.

Yamamuro, Shūhei. 1960. "Oyako kankei—toku ni oya no ishiki ni tsuite" [Parent/child relations—concerning parental mentality in particular]. In Takashi Koyama, ed., *Gendai kazoku no kenkyū* [Contemporary family research]. Tokyo: Kōbundō.

Yanagita, Kunio. 1957. *Japanese Manners and Customs in the Meiji Era.* Translated and adapted by Charles S. Terry. Tokyo: Obunsha.

———. 1967. *Meiji Taishō shi: sesō hen* [A history of the Meiji and Taisho periods: social conditions]. Tokyo: Heibonsha. Originally published in 1931.

Zengoren sanjūnenshi henshū iinkai. 1978. *Kagayakeru zengoren sanjūnenshi* [Thirty-year history of the National Gojokai Federation]. Tokyo: Zenkoku kankonsōsai gojo renmei.

Index

In this Index an "f" after a number indicates a separate reference on the next page, and an "ff" indicates separate references on the next two pages. "Passim" is used for a cluster of references in close but not consecutive sequence.

" adopted " weddings

Shinto weddings = "revival" of trad

22 - Diff b/w ~~the values of~~ what's valued from ♂ + ♀

thru wedding speeches

hierarchy of wedding speakers / guests

busy schedule reference

---

trad + change
change from self-help group to los
(workmen's?)

chapt 6 - Gender

clay / balloon
autonomy / society
indi / group

Library of Congress Cataloging-in-Publication Data

Edwards, Walter Drew, 1949–
    Modern Japan through its weddings : gender, person, and
    society in ritual portrayal / Walter Edwards.
        p.   cm.
    Bibliography: p.
    Includes index.
    ISBN 0-8047-1512-2 (alk. paper)
    ISBN 0-8047-1815-6 (pbk.)
        1. Marriage customs and rites—Japan.   2. Japan—Social life
    and customs—1945–   I. Title.
    GT2784.A2E39   1989
    392'.5'0952—dc19   88-28619
                                                          CIP